# DEVELOPING
# PSYCHODYNAMIC
# COUNSELLING

06

*Developing Counselling*, edited by Windy Dryden, is an innovative series of books which provides counsellors and counselling trainees with practical hints and guidelines on the problems they face in the counselling process. The books assume that readers have a working knowledge of the approach in question, and, in a clear and accessible fashion show how the counsellor can more effectively translate that knowledge into everyday practice.

Books in the series include:

*Developing the Practice of Counselling*
Windy Dryden and Colin Feltham

*Developing Counsellor Supervision*
Colin Feltham and Windy Dryden

*Developing Counsellor Training*
Windy Dryden and Colin Feltham

*Developing Person-Centred Counselling*
Dave Mearns

*Developing Rational Emotive Behavioural Counselling*
Windy Dryden and Joseph Yankura

*Developing Cognitive-Behavioural Counselling*
Michael J. Scott, Stephen G. Stradling and Windy Dryden

# DEVELOPING
# PSYCHODYNAMIC
# COUNSELLING

Brendan McLoughlin

SAGE Publications
London • Thousand Oaks • New Delhi

© Brendan McLoughlin 1995

First published 1995

SAGE Publications Ltd
6 Bonhill Street
London EC2A 4PU

SAGE Publications Inc
2455 Teller Road
Thousand Oaks, California 91320

SAGE Publications India Pvt Ltd
32, M-Block Market
Greater Kailash – I
New Delhi 110 048


**British Library Cataloguing in Publication data**

A catalogue record for this book is
available from the British Library

  ISBN 0 8039 8979 2
  ISBN 0 8039 8980 6 (pbk)

**Library of Congress catalog record available**


Typeset by Mayhew Typesetting, Rhayader, Powys
Printed in Great Britain by Biddles Ltd, Guildford, Surrey

for Fionnuala
and Adam

# Contents

# Preface

In writing this book my purpose has been to address the counsellor who is about to begin to work with clients. I have assumed that she will at least have completed an introductory year and will therefore have some knowledge and understanding of the theory of psychodynamic counselling. Thus what I have to say is not an introduction to the field but rather a discussion about practice. This is not intended as a definitive textbook nor as an exposition of original ideas. Within the limitations imposed by the format, it is an attempt by one practitioner to speak to new colleagues about the transformation of theoretical knowledge into an aesthetic of practice. My hope is that it may encourage the reader to develop her own way of thinking about her work as a psychodynamic counsellor, about the way in which she can begin to hold it all together as a specialized form of relating. As will become clear in the main body of the text, my expectation is that the reader who becomes a counsellor will commit herself to an ongoing dialogue with psychodynamic literature and culture. What I offer here is intended to facilitate that dialogue.

A word is in order about the way in which the book has been written. The format of the book is derived from the series to which it belongs. The need to adhere to that format means that it has not been possible to deal with the various points at great depth. Therefore this is not the book in which to discover all there is to know about transference for example. The reader needs to be prepared to go on reading many other textbooks to develop an in-depth knowledge of a particular topic. What I hope the reader may get from this book is a broad overview of how the counsellor seeks to translate what she is learning into something she can use in a living therapeutic relationship.

Throughout the book I have referred to the counsellor as she and the client as he except in some of the case examples where I have indicated otherwise. I am indebted to those people who have allowed me to use their material to illustrate the points.

As I have already said, I am not claiming to be original in this book and I would like to acknowledge my debt to the many influences on my thinking, through my training, therapy and reading, which have contributed to my own development in the psychodynamic tradition. I am particularly indebted to the many people over the years in whose counselling, therapy, supervision and training I have had the privilege to be involved.

Finally, I would like to thank my wife and son who have supported me in my task and given me time and space to do it, even when they would have preferred me to be with them.

# Introduction

The field of psychodynamic counselling has developed from the psychoanalytic tradition inaugurated by Freud. At its core is a belief in the role of the unconscious in the development of conflict and disturbance. Through the careful unfolding of the therapeutic relationship, within a defined setting, it is understood that resolution of conflict and disturbance may be achieved.

This is chiefly made possible via the agency of the transference counter-transference dynamic, the operation of which focuses the relevant issues between and within the two members of the counselling relationship. Through their commitment to the working through of this relationship, via discourse, attention and interpretation, the counselling couple find their way to a resolution of the client's distress. It is understood that during this relationship the client and counsellor will face anxiety, defence and resistance and that much of the relationship will attend to the painstaking mediation of these difficulties.

Psychodynamic counselling involves the counsellor not as a detached expert but as a primary element in the counselling process and she must therefore be able to rely on her setting to accomplish her task. In this book it is my intention to explore the ways in which the counsellor may develop her own practice of psychodynamic counselling by integrating psychodynamic theory and context. Those readers not yet familiar with the field I would refer to Michael Jacobs's *Psychodynamic Counselling in Action* (1988), also published by Sage. I will begin by discussing some ideas about the psychodynamic context and encounter.

What do I believe myself to be doing when I agree to start a psychodynamic counselling relationship with a client? In the first place I believe I am creating a container in which meaning can be explored and rehearsed. It does seem to me to be a matter of trying out different versions until something seems to fit. To put it another way, until something becomes digestible. Behind this basic idea I see that I am assuming some kind of fundamental exchange between my client and myself.

So how do I think about this container? Clearly it is the consulting room, in the sense of a defined space set apart for the purpose of counselling, including its physical contents, its colours, shapes, textures and smells. I see the room as having particular accents and views, in short a kind of personality, which is in part a reflection of myself and in part a perception of my clients. In any event it is an emotionally laden space which contrives to provide regularity, reliability and security. Perhaps I can say further that I see the consulting room as contributing to the idea of a therapeutic container, matrix, context or space, which is in itself an externalization of such a space within the counsellor. Such an externalization is evidently necessary but I feel it is important to remember that during a counselling relationship, the room is potentially in several different places. It has its own locus in a geographical and temporal sense, but its psychological locus may be the client's inner world or mine, or some representation of my body in its psychological or somatic sense, or potentially some such representation of the client's body or mind. Such considerations may also apply to the waiting room or any other room, e.g. the lavatory, used by the client, as well as the building and street in which they are all located.

The therapeutic container is also a consequence of my behaviour as a psychodynamic counsellor. By adopting a certain way of being and by modelling certain behaviour, I constellate the sense of a contained and containing space. Specifically, I set the boundaries of the relationship in time and space. I say where it will happen and when. I set the duration, the frequency of the sessions and the intervals between them. By the provision and disposition of the consulting room furniture, I orchestrate the space. In doing this I make myself available for use by the client. I invite the use of metaphor rather than literal forms of communication, thus setting frustrations to the acting out of behaviour.

The container is also maintained by the setting of a fee and by the arrangements over such issues as cancellations, missed sessions, holidays and illnesses. Clarity over such issues as place, time, frequency, interval and money, becomes the containing mechanism which allows psychodynamic counselling to begin and to go on. Placing a value on the counselling hour anchors it in reality and signals the need to safeguard the adult realities of both the client and the counsellor. It marks the contractual nature of the agreement, underlining the commitment both parties make to each other and to the pursuit of the counselling. The fee acts as a moderating influence on the omnipotent tendencies of both counsellor and client, and underpins the containing function of psychodynamic counselling by making explicit the professional nature of the contract. A proper level of payment is a safeguard against exploitation in either direction and enables the counsellor to tolerate the extremes of object usage to which the client may subject her.

A further important element in the provision of a psycho-dynamically therapeutic container is, I believe, the theoretical stance and orientation of the counsellor. A practitioner does not just offer a containing space but rather a space which aims at understanding and resolution. To do this the space or container must itself be informed by thinking which, at least in a general sense, seeks to explain experience. Therefore the therapeutic space extends beyond the physical boundaries of the consulting room to occupy a place within the counsellor which is concerned with meaning. The particular elaboration of meaning is the task of every counselling relationship and involves a particular kind of receptivity in the counsellor which allows her to interpret what she receives in ways which together add up to a psychoanalytic worldview. However, the intellectual understanding of what a client says or does in therapeutic space is only one component in the counselling interaction. Equally important is the personal capacity of the counsellor to make herself available for use by the client as one element in a complex form of communication. This requires in the counsellor an openness to emotional and psycho-logical resonances within herself. It is such openness and avail-ability combined with a theoretical matrix, within the setting of a consulting room and a professionally arranged contract, that begins to give the idea of a container in psychodynamic coun-selling its rich and complex meaning (McLoughlin, 1990).

Psychodynamic understanding and theory is based on the work of psychoanalysis and its various developments. It thus becomes possible to speak of a Freudian, Jungian, Kleinian container and so on. These different theoretical orientations are like differing accents and idioms within the same psychoanalytic tongue. As in language generally such differences should never be under-estimated in terms of their impact on the individual's acquisition of linguistic skills. An ability to speak English is no guarantee of a capacity for understanding across the spectrum of regional variations and dialects. Additionally, within a given idiom there is the defining impact of the verbal range and of the voice which gives particularity. Beyond such particularities, which may be thought of as the markers of the individual speaker of a given language, there is surely that additional difference which is the tone of a given relationship.

Thus it seems to me that some aspects of the containing function of the psychodynamic counselling relationship are provided by the generally recognized elements of technique and orientation, which by now we can think of as a culture. Other elements, which to me seem equally important, centre rather more on the person of the practitioner, in physical, psychological and emotional terms. Yet further aspects of the containing function emerge and grow with each counselling relationship, and as such identify a given therapeutic couple; these are aspects which I have already referred to above as tone.

So it seems to me we may think of a psychoanalytic language, which contains a number of dialects and regional variations. We can think of different speakers of psychoanalysis whose accents may be influenced by regional variations, for example the training body, personal therapist or supervisor, on the one hand, and by voice and verbal range on the other, and who in any given psychodynamic relationship find a tone and idiom which belongs to that relationship alone, even if echoes and resonances of other relationships may be heard.

The factors influencing the acquisition of particular linguistic markers are going to be professional and personal. The professional elements comprise the training institute and experience within which a counsellor first learns to speak psychoanalysis. The personal will comprise of all the individual variations which make up a particular person's experience of life. Between the professional and the personal lies the practitioner's own experience of being a client, which brings together what I have called above elements of dialect and tone. Through becoming a client herself the practitioner is enabled to develop her own authentic voice.

The client, of course, brings his own language and story into the therapeutic space and the counsellor will learn from him how he perceives and experiences before she will be ready to speak to him about himself. By meeting him within the psychodynamic container the counsellor will engage the client in a relationship which will develop in him new capacities for thought and understanding.

Thus we have space and we have language. I now want to go on in the rest of this book to look at how the psychodynamic counsellor makes use of the therapeutic container in her relationship with the client.

# I Developing Work with the Internal and External Setting

# 1 Establish and maintain the therapeutic setting

It will be clear from the Introduction that the physical setting in which psychodynamic counselling takes place is an important matter and the responsibility of the counsellor (Storr, 1979). Whether you are working in your own room or in a room provided by an agency, you are trying to contrive a therapeutic space. A first consideration is the integrity of the room, that is, the extent to which it is free from intrusion or impingements from outside or from within. External impingements might be noise in adjoining rooms or perhaps the telephone ringing during a session. Clearly the phone should never be answered while a session is in progress since to do so would be to break the integrity of the therapeutic container. If there has to be a phone in the room it might be best to unplug it. If noise from outside the room becomes intrusive it may be necessary to take steps to address the problem with those responsible. However, only in exceptional cases would it be appropriate to interrupt the session to deal with the intrusion. In the first instance it is better to wait to assess the impact of any external impingement on the client before raising the matter yourself.

It is possible that the source of impingement may be within the counselling room. For example, a counsellor may introduce family photographs or perhaps posters that indicate a particular religious or political stance. While it may be helpful, especially in institutional settings, to give a room a personal note, it is a disturbance of therapeutic space for there to be accidental disclosures about the counsellor's life.

If you are working in your own room it will be simple enough to maintain the character of the room. You will choose and arrange the furniture and the decoration. You will also be able to safeguard the reliability of the setting by ensuring that the room and its contents are not subject to unnecessary changes. For example, you will ensure that the chairs that you provide for your own and your client's use are not removed from the room, nor moved about in it. These may seem small matters but they are in fact significant elements in the maintenance of a therapeutic setting. It may be helpful to remember the complex nature of the therapeutic relationship which finds its expression in both inner and outer reality. If we invite our clients to enter the multi-layered space of the therapeutic setting, they rely on us to ensure the security and reliability of that setting. When we fail to do so by not attending to the constancy of the room and its contents, we simply provoke the resistance of the client and his withdrawal from the therapeutic relationship.

If you are counselling in a room in an institutional setting, it will be important to check things out before the client arrives. Other counsellors may prefer a different disposition of the furniture or lighting in the room. Take time in advance of the session to make sure you are comfortable with the room and that things are as you want them to be. For example, is there a clock in the room and can it be easily seen? As counsellor it is your job to hold the pace of the session and you want to be able to do this without making your client feel that you are clock-watching.

These are of course basic matters, but as you will see throughout this book, consistent and professional attention to things that are basic will develop and enhance your ability to practise.

## Case examples

A male counsellor is working in an agency setting. Additional rooms have been created by converting the top floor of the building. A client already established in counselling is moved to one of the new rooms. The client is a woman of 25, who does not find it easy to trust people and who finds the reality of other people difficult to acknowledge. She arrives for the first session in the new room and settles herself in the normal way. She makes no direct allusion to the change of room but becomes angry when she hears the sound of a typewriter coming from along the corridor.

*Client*: If I can hear the typewriter so clearly, surely they can hear me?
*Counsellor*: [*trying to reassure the client and also deal with his own discomfort over the new arrangements*] I think you'll find that we are speaking too quietly to be overheard.
*Client*: You're lying. I knew I couldn't trust you. There's someone out there listening. You don't care.
*Counsellor*: The change of room is disturbing. You haven't had time to settle into it yet. The sound of the typewriter makes you feel the room may not be suitable for counselling and that by moving you here, I'm showing that I don't care about you.

Here the counsellor is trying to do too much at once, probably because he has been put on the defensive by the client's attack and because the client has unconsciously addressed some of his own ambivalence about the move.

*Client*: You don't care. If you did you would not have moved me here!
*Counsellor*: [*allowing some time for reflection*] The sounds from outside the room make you feel unsafe and remind you of how difficult it is for you to feel that you are safe from intrusion.
*Client*: [*angrily*] That's right!
*Counsellor*: [*tuning in to what he knows from previous material*] When people push you around and dominate you, like when you were a child or when you are at work, you feel bad and that you don't matter. I think you feel the move here is like being pushed around and that it must mean that you don't matter to me either.
*Client*: That's how it always was, somebody else calling the shots.

In this example we can see the disturbing impact of change on both the client and the counsellor. Because he is not yet accustomed to the room and because of his own unresolved feelings about having to move, the counsellor is initially unable to hear what the client is actually telling him. It is only when he has allowed himself time to listen to the client's unconscious prompting that he turns his attention to her experience of being used and to the way in which this is being evoked by the move to a new setting.

In the second example we see how the client directs her female counsellor's attention to the arrangement of the room, in order to feel more connected with her. The client is a woman in mid-life who is no longer sure of her direction, suffers chronic and severe pain and is very depressed. The consulting room is quite large and the chairs are arranged in front of two french windows to the side of the room.

*Client*: I feel this room is so large and formal. You seem to be a long way from me. I want to talk about some of the problems at home but I don't feel I can begin.
*Counsellor*: You feel something about the room gets in the way of you talking?
*Client*: I don't know, I don't feel I can reach you. You seem so far away, so cold and impersonal. [*Long pause*] Perhaps if the chairs were either side of the fireplace rather than in front of the windows, I wouldn't feel so far away.

In this particular case the counsellor tried a number of interpretations to try to deal with her client's difficulty but without success. When it seemed that the counselling might founder over the question of coldness and distance, she took her client's suggestion and placed the chairs either side of the fireplace but at the same distance as before. The client warmed to the new arrangement and the counselling was able to go further.

While it may not often be practicable to rearrange the consulting room to suit every client, this case illustrates the fundamental importance of getting the therapeutic setting right. It also demonstrates that as counsellors we have to make ourselves available to meet our clients before we can sensibly begin to interpret their material.

---

**Key point**

The physical environment in which psychodynamic counselling takes place should not be taken for granted or ignored. Sensitive management of the constancy of the counselling room and attention to the client's relationship to it provide valuable references to the therapeutic dialogue.

---

# 2 Cultivate and develop your therapeutic stance

Having got the setting right the question arises as to how you should conduct yourself within it. The essence of psychodynamic counselling is that the counsellor should make herself available for the client's use in ways that become accessible for interpretation. The idea of the blank screen, so often associated with the psychoanalytic tradition, does not always meet the needs of a particular client, as we saw in the previous point. Clearly then, the practitioner needs to be flexible within a defined setting. She will move within that setting enough to indicate to the client her capacity for genuine involvement at conscious and unconscious levels and to a point where it becomes possible for her to address the client in terms that bring relief.

The therapeutic stance of a psychodynamic counsellor might be thought of as available reserve. By this I mean that the counsellor certainly agrees to meet the client at meaningful levels but she does so without intruding herself in that meeting. In practice, I believe this means that the counsellor holds herself at a respectful distance, facilitating the client's entry into therapeutic space but not directing it. This respectful distance allows the counsellor the space she needs to pay attention to the client as he enters the setting. She will allow him to settle himself in his own way and accept that in doing this he has already begun to communicate within the therapeutic relationship. The counsellor actively attends to the impact of the client's behaviour and his words without immediately responding. In a sense she gathers the impressions the client offers her of himself and allows these to speak to her at different levels. The client may be saying very little or speaking a great deal, by reserving a space within herself to attend to his communication, the counsellor actively listens for the key concern. The reliability and consistency of her attention encourages the client to feel held within the therapeutic relationship.

An underlying assumption in psychodynamic counselling is that the client will seek to place himself or parts of himself within the counsellor, just as he may defend himself against the counsellor trying to do the same to him. The therapeutic stance of attentive reserve is an important element in the counsellor's technique, allowing her to monitor the interplay of the client's inner world with her own and vice versa. It is out of this monitoring process that the counsellor seeks to understand the distress of the client at unconscious levels and attempts to speak to him about it through her interpretations. Thus the therapeutic stance of the psychodynamic counsellor is not an arbitrary device but an integral aspect of her technique which supports her in the extremely difficult task of attending to her client at the different levels at which he presents himself.

For these reasons the psychodynamic counsellor waits before responding to direct questions about herself or about the counselling process. She does not seek directly to comfort a client in distress, just as she does not advise or direct a client what to do. It has been shown that accurate empathy, non-possessive warmth and genuineness are vital elements in any therapeutic relationship (Truax and Carkhuff, 1967). It seems to me that these are all elements of what we are referring to here as the therapeutic stance required for the psychodynamic counsellor. In any counselling orientation the counsellor demonstrates by her behaviour the nature of the therapeutic container that she is offering. The consistency of the reserve and the attention, and the relevance of the interpretations which arise out of these, communicate to the client that she is reliably held and thus facilitate the development of the counselling relationship. When the counsellor's therapeutic stance is altered or wavers she provokes the insecurity of the client and so promotes resistance. Just as the external elements in the therapeutic setting need to remain constant, so the internal consistency of the counsellor's behaviour and responses is required for the client to feel that he can give his trust. A counsellor, of course, does not remain insensitive to the suffering of her client but she uses her feeling responses to help her understand him so that she can begin to talk to him in a way that helps him to begin to understand himself.

## Case example

A very disturbed young woman, psychologically abused by her parents, is seen in an institutional setting by a female counsellor. Sometimes she is silent and looks away, at others she says a great deal, almost overwhelming her counsellor with detail. In a session in which she has been particularly talkative, touching on problems with money, housing, sex and betrayal, she suddenly asks a question, 'Have you read *The Psychopathology of Everyday Life*?' [Freud, 1901], a copy of which is clearly visible on the shelf. She goes on to say, 'I have, in order to catch you out! I started out today with my umbrella but decided on the way that it was silly as there is no rain. I have to go shopping after the session and so I've hidden it behind the door along the corridor. Will it be alright there?' The counsellor waits before responding. She knows that the theme of the umbrella has appeared in this client's material before, sometimes forgotten, sometimes lost, and in one dream, hung outside her bedroom window to hide it from her parents. Even without the prefatory question about Freud's book, the counsellor is aware that this is a complex request.

The umbrella may or may not have been safe hidden behind the door and the counsellor avoids being caught out with a simple answer. She replies, 'I do not know if it will be safe, as I cannot protect what happens outside the room. But perhaps your question is really to do with the fact that you often use your umbrella to refer to yourself and what you are really anxious to know is whether what you leave of yourself here with me will be safe?' The client confirms the counsellor is on the right track by reminding her of the dream and by saying that she thinks of the umbrella as being something capable of extension or potential, like a butterfly.

By avoiding immediate answers to direct questions, in a session already full of material, the counsellor gives herself time to consider what the client is actually asking her. On two occasions the client seeks to draw the counsellor from her stance by her questions. In doing so she tests out the reliability of the counsellor to stay with her task. By avoiding the trap and addressing the underlying anxiety, the counsellor helps the client to make her own links and connections.

---

**Key point**

The counsellor's own behaviour and demeanour are key elements in the provision and maintenance of a therapeutic stance. A counsellor needs to allow herself sufficient detachment from her client if she is to be able to respond to him rather than merely react.

---

## 3   Negotiate and articulate clearly the therapeutic contract

In the foregoing points we have been considering the way in which the formal setting of the counselling room and the formal aspects of the counsellor's behaviour contribute to establishing a therapeutic container within which psychodynamic counselling may take place. A third and equally important element in establishing the idea of a container is the clear negotiation and articulation of the therapeutic contract.

At one level the therapeutic contract is an ethical requirement which provides an explicit framework within which the two parties agree the terms on which they meet (IPC, 1994). Beyond that, I believe that the therapeutic contract also sets the parameters of the counselling relationship at the level of external reality and so provides a necessary differentiation for both client and counsellor for their mutual involvement with inner world reality.

Ethically it is necessary to have a clear contract since any counselling relationship involves itself with the dependence and vulnerability of the client. In my own view the counsellor may also be subject to her own areas of dependence and vulnerability and so also needs the support and protection of a clear contractual understanding. The principal function of the contract from a therapeutic point of view, however, is that it contains the counselling couple in a framework which provides clear markers in terms of their mutual responsibilities.

The counsellor delineates for the client the terms on which she offers to make herself available to him. She does this at the outset of the counselling and so inaugurates her commitment to him. By accepting the terms the counsellor has offered, the client chooses to commit himself to working in a particular way. One of the frequent complaints of the client is about the limited nature of what the counsellor offers. It is an important consideration in assessing a client's suitability for psychodynamic counselling to take into account his capacity to tolerate the limitations of what is on offer. From the counsellor's point of view the limitations set by the therapeutic contract and the client's capacity to tolerate these, are the essential safeguard of her own capacity to do the work of counselling.

In specific terms psychodynamic counsellors negotiate and articulate the therapeutic contract in the areas of time, money and behaviour. The usual practice with psychodynamic counselling is that the client is seen once a week, for a fifty minute session, at the same hour each week. The counsellor will make it clear to the client, once a time has been agreed, that this time is set aside for the client until it is no longer required. By doing this the counsellor is making it clear that it is her intention to remain available to the client for as long as he should need it, setting aside 'a time of your life' as the psychoanalyst Meltzer (1967) has put it. She is thus inviting the client to experience therapeutic space as extending as far into the future as he may need. At the same time the counsellor will indicate her intention to charge for the session whether or not the client attends. In saying this the counsellor is making a very important statement about the continuity of the counselling relationship and about the reality of herself as a separate person, notwithstanding any need the client may have to deny this once the counselling becomes established. The counsellor will also make clear her practice over such issues as holidays and over variations in the rhythm of the work. Knowing that time in the unconscious is not bound to be sequential or linear, the counsellor offers clarity about time as a way of providing a reliable matrix within which she and the client may work.

In setting the fee the counsellor may have to take into account her own need to earn a living, or if she is working in an agency, its need to cover the costs of the service being provided. In either case she needs to recognize the function of the fee as the marker of adult reality. A psychodynamic counselling relationship will inevitably involve some degree of regression to infantile states and therefore to primitive levels of interaction for both members of the counselling couple. Clarity about the fee, together with an appropriate level of remuneration, are important safeguards in maintaining the adequacy of the therapeutic container. This is not to say that the counsellor may not be flexible about setting the fee, but she needs to recognize the reality of the costs that she herself will incur in working with any particular individual at the emotional and psychological level, if she is to avoid becoming personally overdrawn or even bankrupt.

While psychodynamic counsellors do not usually make explicit reference to behaviour within the counselling setting, the thera-peutic stance of the counsellor, as discussed above, models from the outset a way of behaving which discourages acting out while inviting uninhibited exploration in words of whatever may arise (Sandler et al., 1973). In this way, the counsellor articulates for her client the parameters of the psychodynamic model. From the first assessment meeting the counsellor will explore the client's capacity to receive and make use of an interpretation as opposed to discharging his emotion in physical ways or explaining his actions in concrete terms. By doing this the counsellor confronts a key anxiety in the prospective client: is it going to be safe for me to work with you, and is it going to be safe for you to work with me? The psychodynamic approach to counselling seeks to make available to the client the possibility of working effectively with inner world issues that may be terrifying or unthinkable and it does this in the first instance by articulating a contract which replaces action with metaphor, which contains experience within manageable units of time while being linked to each other in continuity, and which is costed realistically between both parties so that neither of them risks being pushed into emptiness.

By being clear about the fee and other practical arrangements, the counsellor is also inviting the client to experience her within the transference. Thus it is not simply a matter of money or time or space but of creating the context within which the transference may be evoked and focused.

## Case example

A recently qualified counsellor is setting up her own practice and decides to continue the custom of her training agency which was not to charge clients who gave notice of a missed session. She tells herself that this seems a fair arrangement. However, as time goes on difficulties emerge. In particular, a businessman client frequently cancels at short notice. In supervision she complains about the disruption to the counselling and also about the loss of income the cancellations involve.

In discussion with her supervisor it emerges that she feels uncomfortable about charging for sessions the client fails to attend as it seems she is charging for nothing. The supervisor points out that she has in fact committed herself to be there for the client, whether or not he turns up. He knows that the session time represents earning time for the counsellor since if he had turned up she would have charged him. He also knows that counselling is long term and ongoing and so it is not possible for the counsellor to put someone in his place. This man's material contained quite a bit of sadism and the supervisor points out that it seems the counsellor has given him power over her by letting him know it is okay for him to decide when he turns up and therefore when he will pay.

The guilt the counsellor feels about charging for missed sessions is an indication that she may still have some unresolved issues of her own about greed, power and self-worth that it will be important for her to resolve in her own therapy. Having done that it will become easier for her to be clear about the purpose of the fee. It may be noted that by telling the client that missed sessions will not be charged for, the counsellor may convey to her client that he does not really matter to her, she can manage without him. In this case the frequent cancellations would be an expression of the client's feelings of worthlessness. In either case the counselling relationship is not being valued and the client begins to act out.

---

### Key point

Clarity about time, money and behaviour at the outset of the counselling relationship provide the counsellor and the client with clear reference points which allow both to explore the unconscious significance of issues relating to the contract.

# 4 Identify and assess your client's inner world position

Whether it is your task to do the initial assessment or you receive someone else's notes, it will be necessary for you to identify and assess your client's inner world position. We can think of a client presenting himself for psychodynamic counselling on two levels. On the first level he presents himself more or less as he is in external reality. On the second level he presents himself as he is in his inner world. The counsellor will, of course, address herself to both levels, but her primary focus must be on where the client is in his inner world. This is both a developmental and a dynamic consideration. Developmentally a client inhabits a particular inner world position and dynamically he operates and interacts from that position. Without an understanding of where a client is in inner world terms the psychodynamic counsellor cannot hope to help her client come to terms with outer world realities.

Essentially this is a question of diagnosis, that is of being able to interpret what a client says in terms that place him within a particular model of understanding, which in this case is, of course, psychodynamic (Hinshelwood, 1991).

Is the client in a world of his own, that is, a world where he has no real awareness of others? Is he perhaps locked in a world where there are just two people, or does he seem sensitive to more complicated relationships? Does the client allow you any room in his discourse, waiting for your responses, or does he cram all the space with his own words? Where does the client seem to locate you? Does he leave you comfortably within your therapeutic stance or does he seem to incorporate you somehow within himself, as if not recognizing your separateness? By asking questions such as these the counsellor supports herself in her difficult task of meeting the client. She gives herself teeth, as it were, which allow her to break down and to begin to digest the unconscious impact of her client's discourse. Without such attempts at discernment, she leaves herself open to being overwhelmed by the impact of her client's inner world. Without any diagnostic assessment of where she will find her client, she runs the risk of not meeting him at all but of attempting to address him from a developmental position he has not yet reached. I well remember a senior psychiatric registrar having a very stern talk with a young male patient in a case conference about him using his undoubted intelligence to pull himself together and to get on with life. He seemed rather baffled when I later pointed out that the young man, who had a narcissistic personality disorder, and therefore lived in his own world, was in no position to agree to do anything.

By assessing the client's inner world position and by continuing to do so throughout the course of the counselling, the counsellor helps to locate her own position in relation to the client and to identify the use to which he is likely to subject her. This kind of awareness on the counsellor's part will help her to tolerate better the impact of the counselling relationship on her own inner world and will make her less likely to act out any retaliatory feelings which may arise. At the same time the continuing attention to assessment helps the counsellor to monitor the progress of the therapeutic relationship and her client's development within it. It will be much easier to differentiate between attempts to break off the counselling and appropriate moves towards an ending, if the counsellor has monitored progress in the client's inner world. It will also be easier for the counsellor to contain the impact of the counselling on herself if she has some sense of where she is in relation to the client. It can be stressful and perhaps even frightening attempting to receive the rage or terror of an adult client, and perhaps, without any diagnostic sense of where he is in his inner world, it may not be very wise. When we agree to make ourselves available for use by the client in therapeutic space, it is our duty both to that client and to ourselves to do so with our minds as well as our hearts. It is well understood within the psychoanalytic tradition that the practitioner must be prepared to experience and, some would say, treat the client's inner world distress within herself before she can begin to help the client with it (Bollas, 1987). This being so, it is necessary for the counsellor to develop the use of her diagnostic and assessment skills, as well as her feeling capacities.

### Case example

A young man comes into counselling because of concerns he has about his capacity to sustain relationships. He talks without pause throughout the session, giving detailed accounts of his conversations with his girlfriend and of their behaviour together. Whatever the counsellor begins to say to him he interrupts, filling up all the space in the room with his anxieties and concerns about the relationship. He finds it intolerable to think of her being apart from him and endlessly reiterates things they have said and done together. The counsellor listens intently to all that is said but finds it difficult to find a purchase on the material, as if there is no way in for her. At a feeling level the counsellor recognizes that she is in danger of being overwhelmed by this client and realizes she needs to find some way of beginning to think about the material. In trying to assess where he might be in inner world terms she takes account of two things. The first is the apparently fused nature of the relationship he describes with his girlfriend. It does come across as if there is only one of them. The second is the impact the client is having on her. He really seems to leave her no room at all, as if he will not allow enough space to develop between them for the counsellor to say anything and therefore for him to experience her as separate.

Thus while he does not make it easy for her to function as a counsellor, by reserving a space within herself to assess what is going on she begins to be able to identify where the client is. Diagnostically she may think of him as being in a primary undifferentiated state and, therefore, still unable to tolerate separateness. She also knows therefore, that for the time being she must expect to be incorporated into his inner world and to be treated as if she had no separate existence of her own. Knowing this will help her to survive the use he makes of her as well as preparing her to begin to address the problems of separation and loss sensitively as they become accessible.

If she were not able to offer herself this diagnostic assessment she might find it increasingly difficult to tolerate the use he will need to make of her and would unconsciously sabotage the counselling relationship, provoking an ending.

---

**Key point**

It is not enough for the psychodynamic counsellor to say this client is unhappy and needs my help. She needs to orientate herself to where the client is dynamically and developmentally so as to be able to address him congruently, and she needs to continue to assess his position throughout the counselling relationship.

# 5   Assess your client's availability for a therapeutic alliance

The term therapeutic alliance refers to that agreement between the counsellor and the client to work together in counselling. It differs from the therapeutic contract which, as we have seen, addresses the parameters of the counselling relationship at both internal and external levels. The therapeutic alliance is about that intention of the client and the counsellor to allow their relationship to be therapeutic. While it is not explicitly articulated, it is as if both parties agree that whatever happens between them they will seek to understand it in terms which will serve the underlying therapeutic aim of the counselling (Sandler et al., 1973).

It must be assumed, though it cannot always be taken for granted, that the counsellor will cooperate in the alliance. It remains a therapeutic task to assess whether or not a given client is available for such an alliance. The psychodynamic counselling relationship is likely to put considerable stress on the client as well as the counsellor. It becomes necessary, therefore, to make an alliance with the client at the outset which will support both parties in their task. The alliance has nothing to do with the counselling couple liking each other or having good feelings about each other, however helpful such feelings may be initially. It is about some part of the client being available to agree to tolerate the strains and frustrations of the therapeutic relationship so that he can stay with it and permit the counsellor to do her work.

At times the client may have to struggle with powerful feelings of resistance which at their most acute will be expressed in the wish to break of the counselling. If a good therapeutic alliance has been established it will be easier for the counsellor to address the resistance and help the client through it. Without a therapeutic alliance the client will almost certainly leave.

For me, the concept of the therapeutic alliance implies that the client has the capacity to split himself between a part which undergoes the counselling and participates in it and a part which recognizes his need to do this and therefore allies itself with the counsellor. If he has been able to enter this alliance he will be free to struggle with the counsellor, presenting his defences and resistance for interpretation and resolution. Without this capacity for an alliance he has no recourse except to resist the whole enterprise. The old joke about counselling goes like this: 'How many counsellors does it take to change a light bulb?' The answer, of course, is 'One, but the bulb has to want to change!' What this joke throws light on is the requirement in counselling for cooperation, that is for some area in the counselling relationship where the counselling couple agree to think about their relationship and the impact they have on each other in terms that connect the counselling with past and current areas of the client's life. It is this agreement which allows the couple to take an 'as if' approach to what happens between them and thus allows them both to tolerate and to survive a great deal. Without this underpinning of the therapeutic relationship in the therapeutic alliance, the intensity of their encounters becomes too acute and there is nothing to stop them destroying each other.

A client's availability for engagement in the therapeutic alliance may vary during the course of the counselling relationship and it is therefore necessary for the counsellor to monitor her client's position in relation to the alliance as the counselling proceeds. I think it can be said that there are times when the counsellor must hold the alliance for both herself and the client, as for example when a client becomes very regressed, but it must never happen that no one is holding the therapeutic alliance. At such a point the relationship would be in danger of becoming mutually destructive, and if it is not possible to recover the position, the relationship should be ended.

In thinking about the internal and external setting of psychodynamic counselling we are paying attention to the delicate balance which must obtain when two people agree to engage with each other in therapeutic space. It is because all the elements within the therapeutic container may potentially represent any or all of the other elements, or become merged or confused, that it is essential to attend to such questions as the therapeutic alliance and the capacity of both the client and the counsellor to maintain their involvement in it.

### Case examples

A male client of 17 is seen in an agency setting by a young male trainee counsellor. The young client presents with difficulties in knowing who he is or what direction his life is taking. He is an anxious and timid young man, clearly suspicious of counselling and the counsellor.

*Client*: I didn't go into college all week.
*Counsellor*: Why not?
[*Long pause*]
*Client*: The other guys.
*Counsellor*: What about the other guys?
[*More silence*]
*Client*: They all seem more together. Like they know what they're doing. I want to be like that. I'm afraid they will laugh at me.
*Counsellor*: You feel drawn to these other guys, attracted by them, but you're worried they'll think you're weak and reject you. I think you face the same problem here, you feel attracted to me and would like to be close, but you worry that I would reject you too.
[*Long silence till the end of the session.*]

The client was then absent for several sessions and it later emerged that he had withdrawn to live on a haystack on his own. The exceptionally dramatic response to the counsellor's remarks is certainly unusual, but it illustrates what happens when transference interpretations are made in the absence of a therapeutic alliance. The problem here was that this interpretation sounded like a seduction. It addressed far too openly the still unconscious homosexual aspects in the young man's transference at too early a stage in the counselling relationship. Because the therapeutic alliance had not had time to become established the young man had no alternative but to receive the counsellor's remarks at a concrete level, which clearly disturbed him and he fled.

A married woman comes into counselling because of a wish to resolve conflicts in her relationship with her father. Following the Christmas break she returns with a heavy cold and not knowing what to talk about. After a while she remarks that she had had a dream about the counsellor (who is male) during the break but she is somewhat embarrassed to talk about it. None the less she tells the dream. 'I am bringing my daughter for an educational assessment and the assessor turns out to be you. I do not want you to talk to her so I take you to one side and seduce you. You seem very passive and I am frustrated as you do not respond.' The counsellor begins by asking the client for associations to the dream. She replies readily. 'I feel very anxious in the dream that you should not get a different picture of me by talking to my daughter, so I decide to seduce you. Whenever I have a sexual dream it always seems to be the same, the man doesn't respond and I feel that it is my fault.'

After some reflection the counsellor remarks: 'It seems that it is very important to you to be able to control how I respond to you. When I fail to succumb to your seduction in the dream you are left feeling powerless and frustrated.' The client responds: 'Yes, I just feel blocked.'

In this case it is possible for the counsellor to make direct reference to the sexual content of the material without provoking resistance. The client has shown her willingness to overcome her resistance by telling the dream. She also shows through her associations her capacity to think about its meaning at other than concrete levels.

Thus in the second example the therapeutic alliance has become adequately established to make it safe for the counsellor to interpret the material with reference to the transference.

---

**Key point**

It is important that the counsellor should not rush into a counselling relationship without taking time to ensure that the client is able to give his consent to a therapeutic alliance and is prepared to allow the counsellor to maintain it.

---

# 6 Abandon memory and desire in relation to your client

The heading for this point is taken from the work of Bion (1967). It is not an invitation to go naked into the counselling relationship, but a suggestion to put aside intentionality, whether of motive (for example, I care), or aim (I want to take away your depression) in favour of availability. Being there, for and with the client, allows for communication which leads to the possibility of digestion and interpretation which in turn may lead to resolution and relief.

It may seem rather like a mystical injunction to the practitioner whereas in fact it is nothing of the kind. Bion's emphasis is on the practice of a very precise kind of attention which does not allow itself to be distracted by too much striving. As soon as you turn your attention to getting something right, to being especially understanding or to framing exactly the right interpretation, you have left therapeutic space and have entered some unconsciously formed realm of your own.

The counsellor at the beginning of her practice is often concerned that she will not be able to hold her clients in her mind. The trainee in supervision is anxious to record every detail of the session and so win the supervisor's approval. Undoubtedly, it takes time, experience and growing confidence in her skills as a practitioner for the counsellor to be able to relax in the way that Bion's injunction implies. What does eventually happen is that increasing experience shows the counsellor that what she requires to be effective is not a detailed memory but a respect for and faith in the psychodynamic process itself.

You do not have to search your memory or strive to be in charge of the counselling. What you do need to do is to pay consistent and reliable attention to all that is going on between you. You observe how the client behaves, you listen to all he says, you assess his impact on you, you attend to your own feelings and thoughts, you keep track of where you seem to be located in relation to each other and you monitor the fate of your own interventions and interpretations. Thus if you are so acutely present to all that is going on in the therapeutic exchange you have no time to concern yourself with what was said last time or with hoping that your client is getting better.

In saying this I am not suggesting that you can forget what your client tells you, or that it does not matter whether you care about him or not. What I am saying is that while you are counselling you have to empty your mind of all kinds of distractions if you are to have a realistic chance of hearing what your client is saying to you now. Thus when we take detailed notes of a session, as for example for supervision purposes, it is not so that we do not forget what was said, though that can be important, but so that we can accurately follow what may have been going on in the room between the counselling couple. It is not simply the task of counselling to uncover what is unconscious, or to elucidate what may have happened in the past. It is also a therapeutic task for the counsellor to be available to her client in the here and now and to receive his discourse accurately and authentically. It is usually anxiety to do her best or to get it right that prevents the counsellor from being there both to receive what the client is telling her and to digest what is being said within herself in response. However, it is precisely in the interface between the client – counsellor interaction that the therapeutic work of psychodynamic counselling is actually done. Where the counsellor has become preoccupied or distracted with her own concerns to get something right or to help a particular kind of client, she is less able to pay attention to this interface and thus reduces her chances of understanding her client and, therefore, of being able to talk to him about himself.

Clients will often begin a session by stating they cannot remember what they were talking about last time. Sometimes this is done in such a way that the counsellor feels under severe pressure to supply the forgotten link. If possible the counsellor needs to resist this kind of pressure and to turn her attention instead to what the client is trying to tell her by starting in this way. It may be that the client in starting in this way is trying to speak about the idea of something or someone being forgotten, or of losing his sense of connectedness between things. If the counsellor is less distracted by her own needs and wishes she is more likely to attend to the core of what the client is saying and to respond appropriately.

## Case example

A counsellor reports in supervision about the particular difficulty she is having in working with a young woman client who has recently come into counselling with acute depression. The woman invariably starts the session by stating how awful she feels and what a bad night she has had:

> 'I feel dreadful. I wish I didn't have to feel like this. I hate where I'm living. I feel so cut off. I've lived in some terrible places. I always seem to have problems with the landlord. We moved around so much when I was young. I always seemed to be the odd one out. They used to make fun of my accent. Perhaps I did use to speak funny. It just made me feel lonely. It's such a long way on the bus. I can't see the point of getting up.'

Such monologues continue without pause and the counsellor reports that she finds herself realizing she is unable to remember what the client has been saying:

> 'I just don't seem to be able to hear what she is saying to me. She just goes on and on and I end up only being able to lamely reflect back the last thing I heard and I'm not always sure what I heard. I think I feel bored and that she's just going to go on complaining and that it will never stop. I don't think I'm doing her much good. I can't hold on to anything she says.'

The supervisor deals with the counsellor's concerns by saying:

'Holding on to what she says may not be the important thing at the moment but rather paying attention to what is happening between you in the room. If you find you cannot remember what she said to you five minutes ago then stop trying and turn your attention instead to how she makes you feel. Tune in to your boredom and to your fear that it will never stop and try to talk to your client about her anxiety that things may never be any different.'

But the counsellor is worried that the client will feel let down if the counsellor cannot remember what she's just said. The supervisor replies that:

'She will feel let down if you allow yourself to become paralysed by your inability to remember. But if you pay attention to the impact she is having on you and talk to her about that, she may feel that here at last is someone who is attending to her. Perhaps then she will feel less panic and may be able to begin talking to you rather than at you.'

---

**Key point**

Anxiety about remembering what the client has said or about getting it right, tends to inhibit the counsellor's ability to give consistent and reliable attention to the client. Staying with the client is more helpful than striving to help him.

---

# II Developing Work with Issues around the Boundaries

# 7 Observe and respond to your client's activities around the boundaries

Having established a sense of the therapeutic setting, the counsellor now has a defined space within which she can meet her client. Because she is clear in herself about that setting she is able to attend to her client's behaviour in relation to the boundaries of the setting. Everything that happens within a therapeutic relationship is an attempt at communication, whether consciously or unconsciously determined, and this is particularly so in relation to activities around the boundaries.

As you hold your stance and observe your client you will see him behaving within the container you have provided. He may seek to insert himself compliantly, doing his utmost to fit in with you. Perhaps he will arrive on the dot and remove himself just as punctually. Alternatively he may arrive very early or very late. At times he may not appear at all and give no warning of his absence. In each instance the client is behaving significantly in terms of the boundaries you have set and therefore invites you to consider the meaning of his behaviour in relation to you. At the outset of your practice it is very easy to be so concerned with your own performance that you miss the efforts of the client to convey something to you through his behaviour.

It is also possible to find yourself interpreting a client's behaviour somewhat personally rather than considering it as a form of communication. Thus the client who fails to turn up may stir up feelings of inadequacy in the counsellor who tends to explain his absence as a reflection on herself. It is far more likely that the client is expressing something about his own problems about being in a therapeutic relationship than any direct reference to the counsellor.

Some clients try to undermine the container by seeking to draw the counsellor from her stance. This may be done by asking frequent and direct questions, perhaps about the counsellor or maybe about the nature of counselling. Still others seek to attack the container by behaving inappropriately, for example by being overtly aggressive or by attempting to seduce the counsellor. It may be helpful to remember, particularly in the initial stages of the counselling relationship, that these boundary issues are usually arising in response to having started counselling and therefore need to be dealt with as expressing resistance to the process. The appearance of apparently aggressive or seductive behaviour may relate to resistance at any point in the counselling relationship but this is not invariably so and the counsellor may need to assess whether she is confronted principally with aspects of resistance or regression. With resistance your aim is ultimately to overcome the anxiety and move on, with regression you are concerned to facilitate the client's working through the position they have reached.

Sometimes boundary issues confront us with very direct questions as to what we should do. For example, if a client arrives early, should you start the session early? If he missed a session because of a rail strike, do you still charge him? A client who has travelled a long way asks for a cup of tea, do you make one? Another client deliberately knocks something over or throws something, do you make him pick it up? Perhaps a client seems very distressed and is causing you concern, do you offer your home telephone number? The spouse or parents of your client contact you, do you talk to them? You are out at the cinema or the supermarket and suddenly you are face to face with your client, do you greet each other? Clearly there could be many more examples and in practice there will be. The answers could conceivably be different with different counsellors or different clients. However, I believe what would remain the same in every case is the overriding importance of maintaining the integrity of the therapeutic container. If something you are asked to do makes it difficult for you to maintain your therapeutic stance and remain true to your role as counsellor, then the answer is simple: don't do it.

With your first cases in training you will of course make mistakes, and through discussion in supervision you will build on these mistakes. Even very experienced counsellors will make mistakes in relation to boundary issues and usually there is some important communication to be understood as a result. However, whenever the boundaries have been crossed by either client or counsellor, it is important that some recognition of this fact is made so that the boundaries may be reinstated.

One of the best examples I know of understanding the importance of having and maintaining boundaries comes from the work of a couple who foster and care for abused children. They had a magic carpet, an oriental rug, usually kept rolled up behind the sofa. Whenever a child needed to talk about or express something particularly difficult, the rug would be brought out and unrolled. The child would then take up its position on the rug and with the absolute knowledge that they had the freedom and safety to do so, would express whatever they needed to get out. Once the session was over the rug would be rolled up and put away until it might be needed again and whatever had emerged on the rug would remain there, unless the child chose otherwise. Without theory or training behind them this couple had understood what every counsellor needs to know, that without a clearly defined container, whose boundaries will be respected, there can be no therapeutic disclosure and no counselling relationship.

## Case example

A professional man who had come into counselling because of stress at work arrived with a party of friends at a restaurant and was conducted to a table adjacent to a couple. As he sat down he recognized the woman as his counsellor and he and she smiled at each other. At the next session he made no reference to the incident and continued talking about work. The counsellor felt she could not let the session end without some attempt to acknowledge what had happened and brought it up herself. The man listened to his counsellor's remarks and then stated that he had not thought about their chance meeting and, therefore, he thought it was not a problem to him. The counsellor accepted his very reasonable response and felt relieved that no harm had resulted. However, as time went on the client increasingly turned up late or cancelled at the last moment. When he did arrive he was often apologetic at having little or nothing to say. This situation went on for some time, the counselling process obviously having stalled, until it occurred to the counsellor to raise again the incident in the restaurant. This time, with the evidence of his obvious resistance to help him, the man was able to acknowledge that their meeting outside the session had indeed disturbed his confidence in the counselling relationship. In particular he realized that he felt unable to control what his counsellor might know about him if it was possible for her to see him outside the session. In this example the counselling process itself had to suffer until it was possible for both the counsellor and the client to allow themselves to attend to the importance of the boundaries.

---

**Key point**

The provision of a clearly determined therapeutic container in psychodynamic counselling permits the counsellor to attend to her client's behaviour around boundary issues as important elements in his communications.

---

# 8   Pay particular attention to beginnings and endings

Much of the difficulty in being in the counselling relationship is for the counsellor to know how to orientate herself in relation to the client. At the outset of the relationship it may seem clear enough why a client is seeking counselling; an experience of loss or depression, difficulties in forming relationships and so on. But what is going on once the counselling has become established? How does the counsellor make sense of what is happening once the presenting problem is no longer the focus of the narrative? Alternatively, where a client seems to have a lot to say about a number of apparently quite different things, how might the counsellor decide what to pick up and what to leave? Paying attention to what transpires at the beginning or at the end of a session is often an important indicator of what matters to the client, even if he remains largely unconscious of it.

As part of my training I undertook the observation of an infant once a week from birth to age 2. As the baby grew older I was often struck by the way in which some activity he had been engaged in at the end of our previous meeting would be immediately resumed at the start of our next. It was as if he came to use the regularity of our meetings, an hour a week at the same time, as a container within which he could work with something, which he would signal at the beginning and ending of each observation. Similarly, the client will often give notice at the extremes of the session of issues which concern him and, therefore, which he needs his counsellor to understand. This may simply be there in the subject matter of the client's discourse, though not necessarily in the content of his words.

For example, a client may end a session by some seemingly lighthearted reference to going back out into the bad weather, or begin a session by explaining his lateness in terms of heavy traffic. In the first instance the client may wish the counsellor to attend to the idea of a break in his experience resulting in something worse for him; in the second the client may be needing to raise his difficulties about things that get in his way. At times it may be more in what the client does than in what he says that points the counsellor in the direction of his concerns. For example, a client who usually anticipates the ending of the session by looking round at the clock may be alerting you to his anxiety that he is boring you, or that time is running out for him. On coming into the room a client sits down and holds the cushion from the chair on his lap. It may be that he is letting the counsellor know that he feels more comfortable when he has something between himself and her, or perhaps that he needs something to hold on to.

It will be apparent that the explanations I have offered in these examples are somewhat arbitrary in themselves. It is not possible to say what a particular action or theme may mean except in its own context and a counsellor will want to wait and attend to what else is going on in the session before reaching a conclusion. Even if the counsellor interprets the events at the beginning and ending of the session correctly, it will not usually be correct to talk about them at once. Most of these communications on the threshold will be largely unconscious for the client and it is important that the counsellor does not try to talk about them before they become accessible to him. In the first instance, therefore, the counsellor will pay attention to beginnings and endings and will gather what may be there to think about and consider. Only when additional material becomes available during the course of the session or over a number of sessions will the moment have arrived for interpretation (Fenichel, 1945). The danger in speaking too soon about your direct observation of the client is that he will simply reject it as fanciful, or if he accepts it, may begin to feel, perhaps with some justice, that he has become the object of your critical attention. For some clients, particularly in borderline cases, this kind of intrusive interpretation may be experienced as persecutory and have a destructive effect.

Sometimes what the client signals at the extremes of the session is not a major disclosure in itself so much as the setting of a theme which it will be important to bear in mind while listening to the rest of the session. Of course it may often happen that a counsellor may feel that she understands very little of what is going on in a particular session or with a particular client. Attending to the beginnings and endings with such cases may often be the only way of finding a way into the material. We should remember that in psychodynamic counselling the client is often struggling to talk about things that may never have been put into words before and which may often begin to be expressed not directly through words, but through events, actions, images themes and so on, which, if given time, may eventually come to form the required words in the mind of the counsellor. It may be that the counsellor herself only achieves a sense of understanding outside the session, for example in supervision or in reading some relevant paper. If she takes her cues from her client's communications around the thresholds, she will be able to make use of her understanding to meet the client where he is. It can also be helpful to consider the client's use of beginnings and endings as a way of making links between the sessions, or of making comments about what he experiences as a lack of links or of discontinuity.

### Case example

A woman in mid-life came into counselling because she was depressed and felt that she had lost her way. Her parents had both worked in medicine, and she would invariably begin her sessions with some reference to her state of health.

'I'm not feeling very well today.'
'I have a migraine.'
'I have a viral infection, everyone seems to have it.'
'I'm feeling terrible, I'm waiting for my period to start.'

As the woman then went on to talk of other things, the counsellor initially paid little attention to these remarks. However, as she listened to the rest of the client's discourse the counsellor began to realize just how much of what she had to say was in the nature of a complaint, which over time became quite difficult for her to hold. Nor did it seem easy, without appearing critical of the client, to begin to address this habit of complaining. The counsellor decided to bring the problem into supervision and began to read through her notes in preparation. As she did so she began to notice the character of the opening remarks and saw that these too were complaints, though about aches, pains and illness. Having begun to pay attention to her characteristic opening remarks the counsellor was able to see that this woman was relating to her in counselling in much the same way the patient does with her doctor. In the next session she was able to pick up the initial complaint in the following way:

*Client*: I'm so tired at the moment, I think I must be run down.
*Counsellor*: I've been thinking about what you tell me about your life and have noticed how much of it seems to be in the form of a complaint.
*Client*: That's how it is.
*Counsellor*: I'm also struck by the way at the beginning of each session you usually tell me how you are feeling physically, as if perhaps you feel you have to justify coming here by presenting me with your symptoms.
*Client*: That's what it's like having doctors for parents. Have you had your bowels opened? Do you have a temperature? There's no problem, you're not ill!
*Counsellor*: And that's what you fear here, if you have no complaints, I might not believe you have any problems?
*Client*: [*tears streaming down her face, nodding*]

---

**Key point**

Psychodynamic counselling is an ongoing discourse. If you allow your attention to dwell on the client's opening and closing communications, you may find him helping you to keep track of where he is.

---

# 9 Allow for the importance and impact of gaps, breaks and interruptions to the counselling

At its most basic we can say that psychodynamic counselling happens once a week at the same time for 50 minutes. There is, therefore, a reliability, a regularity and a rhythm in the experience of such a counselling relationship which provides us with useful markers for our thinking about any variations that may occur. If we remember that the counselling relationship itself invites regression, it may help us to give due weight to the impact of the time spent away from the session.

The first rupture to the experience of therapeutic continuity is inevitably the gap that is there between one session and the next. This is clearly such a given of external reality, no matter what the frequency of the sessions, that it is sometimes easy to forget that it has an emotional quality for the client. For some clients whose ego strengths may not be very great, the gap of a week may seem to present an unsurmountable barrier to making any genuine contact at all and it may be necessary to refer them on. Where this is not the case, the once a week frequency may still present the client with considerable problems in achieving a sense of containment and continuity and the counsellor will need to allow for this in working with the transference. For other clients a once a week contact is not in itself a major issue in terms of their capacity to work. However, even in these cases it is important to allow for the possibility that the experience of the gap between the sessions will begin to carry some important feelings for the client. I think the principle here is that the counsellor becomes as important to the client in his experience of her as absent or elsewhere, as she does in his experience of her presence and of being present to him. Thus while the counselling relationship happens in a particular moment of time and space at an external level, it has a literally ongoing quality at the inner world level.

It is because of this ongoing quality of the counselling relationship that it becomes useful for us to pay attention to variations in its rhythm. Psychodynamic counselling is usually an open-ended, long-term contract, and, therefore, there will inevitably be breaks. On the whole, such breaks will follow the customary pattern of holidays, Christmas, Easter and summer, and will therefore not usually be experienced as simply arbitrary in themselves. What may be experienced as arbitrary is the fact that the counsellor will determine the actual dates and the duration of the break and will usually charge those clients for sessions missed through extending or anticipating the break or through arranging holidays at different times. It is important that notice is given well in advance of any break so that ample time be allowed for dealing with issues that may arise. This is particularly so if there is to be a break which is additional to the expected pauses. Even where time has been allowed in advance, but especially when this has not been possible, time and attention may need to be given after a break to allow for its impact to be felt and expressed.

Even when a break in the counselling comes about as a result of the client's own action, the counsellor may need to allow for the possibility that the break is experienced as stemming from her. Thus even breaks caused by the client may be experienced as absences by the counsellor. Similarly, efforts to reschedule a session because the client is unable to come at the usual time may not have a straightforwardly beneficial effect. The counsellor who is too ready to offer an alternative time to a client who is having to miss a session may be conveying what feels to the client like anxiety about his capacity to survive in her absence. In the same way, failing to charge for a missed session may suggest to the client that this is a take it or leave it kind of arrangement, without any continuity of holding. If the counsellor fails to hold the boundaries for him, confusions and fears about his own separateness or about the viability of his existence are provoked.

## Case examples

A male counsellor is due to become a father in a couple of months' time. He alerts his clients to the possibility that he may have to cancel sessions at short notice around a certain date. He offers no further information. He finds that different clients respond in different ways. The majority receive the information initially without comment, though most return to it in subsequent sessions. After some thought one or two clients ask him directly if a baby is expected. The counsellor confirms their deduction and waits to see what they will do with this news. For some it is an opportunity to express warm positive feelings about the idea of their counsellor becoming a father, with more or less explicit identification with the baby who is to become the object of such loving attention. For others the news is received with more ambivalence, with the expected baby becoming the focus for feelings of envy and rage. In either case it is useful for the counsellor to begin to work with these responses well in advance of the birth of his child, as it gives him time to separate what is happening in the transference from what is happening in his own reality.

Some clients conclude that his announcement about a possible absence at short notice must mean that the counsellor is ill and may need an operation. As this is not the case he is able to reassure them at the level of reality while also taking the opportunity to work with their anxieties in the transference about reliability, loss and separation.

Whatever the fantasy evoked in response to his announcement, it is clear that by anticipating a possible break in the rhythm of the work, the counsellor has created the opportunity to hold his clients through such a break, as well as opening up the transference in different ways for different clients.

In the second example, a young male client who had been abused, telephones the week before the Christmas break in advance of his usual appointment and leaves a message on the machine asking if he could have an additional session before the holiday. On receiving the message the counsellor consults her diary and sees that it will not be possible to agree to the request. She then begins to consider what the urgency for an extra session might be about and whether it would be appropriate to meet the request even if she could. She realizes that even an apparently practical request left on the answering machine needs to be considered as a communication in the transference and therefore considered in its whole context. From this point it is relatively easy for her to see that the request for more time just before the break is likely to have something to do with the client's feelings about the coming gap in the work and that it is from this perspective that she needs to respond. When she does so, the young man, while disappointed at not being able to have the extra session, is clearly relieved to have his feelings about the break opened up and expressed.

---

**Key point**

Psychodynamic counselling involves powerful feelings of attachment in the transference; thus any break in the work, whether or not anticipated or seemingly rationally discussed, represents a potential crisis for the client.

---

# 10 Receive and respond appropriately to your client's signals about money, time and space

We have been thinking about psychodynamic counselling as a relationship which takes place within a context, the boundaries of which permit us to explore the meaning of the client–counsellor interactions. The client's use of space, time and money are three areas which call for such exploration. While a client may know what he wishes to discuss at a conscious level, his behaviour will often disclose another focus for the counsellor's attention which may sometimes need to be received as the primary disclosure. The three areas of money, time and space all lend themselves as metaphors to divulge the client's communications about his experience of himself in relation to others. One or all of these areas may be used to refer to his inner world experience.

Money may be fairly easily seen to signify something that is exchanged between two people, a resource. Therefore it may represent food, power, love, capacity. It may be something that is offered and freely given or something that is hoarded and withheld. It may be received or taken, gift or theft. It is something that can be saved and managed or something that can be squandered and lost. In practice the counsellor will need to pay attention to the responses of the client in connection with the fee and the ritual of payment as well as to what the client may have to say about how he handles money in other areas of his life. It is not a matter of attaching fixed meanings to what a client does with money but of allowing for the use of money as an element in communication.

Time and the client's relationship to it is another way in which important communications may be made. The client, obviously, may be late or early, either way he may seek to have an impact on the counsellor. It is all too easy to receive the rational explanations of the client about traffic and other hold-ups as if they were the last word on the subject. The counsellor may sometimes have to challenge the rational and concrete explanations if she is to break through to the unconscious communication they contain. Attention may also need to be given to the client's use of time during the session since this may also be a way he seeks to impress upon the counsellor some aspect of his inner world experience. With some clients there is that sense of there being no time at all, whereas with others time seems to weigh heavily between you as if there might be no way of using it up. Some clients never seem to allow themselves enough time, lamenting at the end of the session that they have not got round to talking about what they really needed to talk about. Still others seem overwhelmed by the amount of time available as if they could not imagine how to fill it. Whatever a particular client seems to be saying about time, he is inviting the counsellor to understand something about his early experience of time in relation to others as well as how he experiences the current situation with her. Sometimes what the client does with time is quite subtle and once again it is possible for the counsellor to miss what is being conveyed. This is perhaps less likely to occur if the counsellor reminds herself to attend to the idea of meaning beneath the surface of things and beyond the rational explanations that may be offered.

Space is a third element the client may need to use to make something clear to the counsellor. Space is a concept akin to the idea of territory and is something that may be shared, occupied, invaded, laid waste and so on. A client may physically use space in a way which indicates his availability or capacity for relationship. Some clients seem to bring a great deal of paraphernalia into the room with them. They may dispose this tightly around them or perhaps they seek to cover every available surface with some object of their own. I remember one client who would often manage to place some object between me and the clock.

Clients may also make use of their narrative to occupy space in the session. Thus a client may talk rapidly and continuously and thus make the counsellor feel that there is no room for her to be with the client and no gap for her to get into the dialogue. At times the client may succeed in so stuffing the counsellor with material that it is as if there is no space left within the counsellor. The impact of this may be that the counsellor feels she has no space within her where she may reflect on what is happening and digest it. In this way the client has managed to occupy the counsellor and take her over.

The counsellor who has a clear understanding of the significance of space, time and money, is in a better position to receive the signals of her clients in these areas and so respond appropriately by addressing the particular quality of object relationship which they are seeking to disclose.

## Case examples

A woman who had been in counselling for several years and with whom work was moving towards its end began to arrive 10 minutes early for her session. The counsellor worked at home and had no waiting room and so would show the client into the counselling room and withdraw until the due time. While waiting for the session to begin the client would receive the counsellor's cat, which got into the habit of presenting itself for her attentions. By the time the counsellor arrived to begin the session he would find that it was, as it were, already under way, with the cat fostering a very positive transference indeed! As this happened on several occasions it became apparent that the client was dealing with some of her feelings about the ending of the work by extending the session time and becoming intimate with the counsellor's cat.

A young man has come into counselling because of his difficulties in relationships and is seen by a counsellor in training. The client presents himself with considerable vitality and energy, talking endlessly and answering his own questions. On arrival in the room he takes some time to settle in, placing a coat on one chair, a jacket on another and maybe a pullover on the table. Not infrequently he arrives with various bags or sandwiches which he deposits on whatever surface he can find. He refers to his own actions as if offering a commentary. On occasion he enters with a cup of coffee bought from the machine in the waiting room where he has met and interviewed other clients. He seems jovial and it is apparent from his discourse that he engages many other people to listen to his story as well as his counsellor. The counsellor experiences feelings of frustration and annoyance with the client as it seems to her that he leaves her neither space nor time to address him. His physical and verbal invasion of the room speak to her of his anxiety about relating and his need to defend himself by plugging every opening.

A young man who has dabbled with drugs is referred by his girlfriend because of his difficulties in remaining faithful. He does not understand his need to sleep with other women and is distressed by the pain he is causing. From the outset his timekeeping is erratic making his counsellor wonder if the relationship will establish itself or just peter out. He explains that his parents will pay for the counselling as he is still a student. However, when the time comes for settling the bill there appear to be some difficulties. He is not a very organized young man and on the surface it seems that he has simply failed to present the bill to his mother. However, as several sessions elapse and he still does not manage to pay, the counsellor sees that she needs to look more closely at what this is about. She raises with him the unpaid bill and remarks that it seems he is needing to draw her attention to something by repeatedly failing to settle the account. He is then able to begin talking about how difficult he finds it to ask his mother for anything and that while he has always had an allowance he has also frequently felt the need to steal from her purse.

---

**Key point**

The client unconsciously uses whatever means he can to disclose himself to the counsellor who needs to maintain a broad focus of attention in order not to miss his signals.

---

# 11   Recognize the limits of your competence and refer on where appropriate

In order to feel that she may work well and with confidence in her abilities, the counsellor needs to know and to acknowledge that there will be some clients whose needs lie beyond the scope of her competence. While to a certain extent we are all challenged to work at the limits of our competence (Meltzer, 1967), it is important both for the sake of the client and of the counsellor that the counsellor holds open for herself the possibility that she may not be adequately equipped to work with a particular client. Where this happens she needs to feel free to raise the matter with her supervisor and if necessary to refer the client on.

Basically there are likely to be two ways in which competence becomes an issue. One is largely to do with the client while the other has more to do with the counsellor. From the point of view of the client it may simply be that a certain client is more disturbed or more needy than it is possible to hold in a once a week relationship. Clearly this is an issue which should be considered at the time of the initial assessment. However, experience shows that levels of need and disturbance are not always correctly assessed at the outset and in some cases only come to light in response to the stress of engaging in the counselling relationship itself. Also newly qualified counsellors who are beginning to work independently may be tempted to accept referrals in order to establish their practice. They may do this at the expense of making a balanced assessment of the client's needs. Where this happens they may find themselves running into serious difficulties in managing the relationship.

Where a client seems unable to engage in a therapeutic alliance, where they seem unable to tolerate the frustrations of once a week work, where they show little or no capacity for insight or for making use of an interpretation, where they seem to lack any other relationships of any depth, where there is evidence of obsessional or addictive behaviour, the counsellor needs to consider that this particular client may be unsuitable for what she is able to offer (Malan, 1979). It may be that as she develops her experience she may learn to work at greater depth but she should not continue to work with someone whose needs she recognizes to be greater than her competence may meet.

It may be that the difficulty is not so much with the client and his needs but in the counsellor and hers. Psychodynamic counselling is a relationship which puts considerable demands on the counsellor herself. To work effectively she needs to be able to make herself available to the client at various levels. Hopefully her training will require her to become a client herself and so give her the opportunity to work with her own inner world issues as well as experiencing what it is like to be in counselling. Even so, it can happen that a particular client raises challenges for her at a level she has not herself been able to address as a client. In such a case it is unlikely she will be able to work effectively with the client and it may become appropriate for her to refer on. Where a counsellor has had little or no experience of being a client herself, she may be unable to recognize the depth at which the client needs to contact her and may fail to recognize the intensity of the transference. At best she will simply glide over the surface, leaving the client to fend for himself. At worst she will make use of the client to project her own problems and so make his situation worse. Whenever a counsellor begins to feel that she is unable to work with a client she should bring her difficulties into supervision. There she needs to be prepared to identify whether the problem is primarily to do with the inadequacy of the container for the needs of a particular client or whether it is more to do with the difficulties in herself which she needs to address in her own right. In either case she will need to discuss with her supervisor how to handle the referral on of the client whenever this seems to be indicated.

## Case example

A newly qualified woman counsellor is anxious to establish her own practice and agrees to work with a man who presents with depression. The counsellor works in her own home alone. As the counselling becomes established the man begins to talk about his relationships and in particular about his sexual practices and fantasies. Much of what he has to talk about is sadomasochistic in character. In supervision the counsellor initially reports that she is not disturbed by the nature of his material and feels it is not really the main issue with him. However, as time goes on she notices herself becoming unsettled on the days he is due for a session and begins to wonder if it is safe for her to be alone with him in the house. When some difficulties over the timing of the session arise she takes the opportunity to end their work and refers him on to an agency setting.

---

**Key point**

The counsellor owes it to her client and to herself not to pursue a counselling relationship where she recognizes that she is out of her depth. It is healthy to recognize your limits and to refer on.

---

# 12  Resist the invitations of the client to collusion

Nothing is straightforward in human relationships and this is as true for the psychodynamic counselling relationship as it is for any other. As surely as the client seeks help for himself by coming into counselling he will also place obstacles in the way of this help. One of the ways in which the client will do this is to invite the counsellor into collusion. Basically what I mean by this is that the client will seek to establish a spurious sense of intimacy or mutuality from early on in the relationship. Some clients will do this by immediately addressing the counsellor by her first name or by talking in such a way as to suggest that they are both operating from basically the same position.

These clients may seem charming and plausible. They appear rational and cooperative and appear to take an intelligent interest in their counselling. Having come into counselling they spend their time trying to avoid becoming a client. They will seek to draw the counsellor into discussion. They may be quite knowledgeable about the literature and imply that therefore they understand something. What they do not do very readily is genuinely talk about themselves They may talk about other people. Indeed at times such clients will bring very arresting and stimulating material about other people or about world events. By and large, however, they will resist any attempt the counsellor may make to interpret this material as relating to themselves and their inner world situations.

It seems to me that such clients are frightened by the intimacy of the counselling relationship and are likely to be concerned about the possibility of developing feelings of dependence. They seek to avoid their fears by taking control of the counselling relationship and trying to convert it into something else, a discussion, or 'our little chats' as some clients put it. The counsellor needs to resist these invitations to collusion from the beginning as they represent nothing less than an attempt to subvert the whole process. Basically the client's wish is to prevent the counsellor from functioning as a counsellor, to prevent her from thinking about the client and so stop her understanding him. Clearly as such it represents a form of resistance but it is distinguished from other forms in that it actively seeks to involve the cooperation of the counsellor as a partner in the resistance. One of the difficulties for the counsellor in identifying that there is a problem is that the client is so apparently satisfied by what is going on. When so many clients seem so stuck or to be making very slow progress it can be very tempting to enjoy the respite which is afforded by someone who appears to be cooperating. However, as time goes by it is clear that nothing is really being achieved with the client himself.

Where there is an appearance of reasonable rapport with the client alongside an apparent unwillingness to allow anything to refer to himself, it may be that a state of collusion obtains. The counsellor who is able to identify this needs to address it with the client if the counselling is ever to be allowed to do its work. In a sense the counsellor will be trying to renegotiate the therapeutic alliance, and once discovered the client may or may not be able to respond. Where he is not able, the counselling is likely to be terminated.

It is clearly preferable if the client's invitations to collusion are recognized as such from early on. Where they are not it is possible to work together for quite a time without the counselling really beginning. Where this happens, the danger is that the part of the client which recognizes the need for help is abandoned by the collusive alliance between the counsellor and the client. This situation will tend to confirm the underlying anxiety about the safety of the counselling relationship and the situation may be beyond repair.

## Case example

A woman counsellor in training begins work with a woman of a similar age and position in life. The client has been referred by her GP following difficulties arising at work. It seems important to the client that she and the counsellor are of a similar age and she assumes a basic understanding on the part of the counsellor because of this. She expresses the view that women their age have already seen much of life and therefore see things in a certain way. The counsellor finds herself drawn to her client, feeling that there is much that she can agree with and support. The client attends regularly and punctually, enquires always how the counsellor is feeling and generally makes herself agreeable. She speaks readily and much but always about other people or about things in general. What she does not do is give the counsellor any glimpse of how things are for her or what her deeper feelings may be in the counselling relationship. After working together for a couple of months the counsellor begins to feel that as pleasant as the sessions may be, nothing really seems to be happening with this woman. She is particularly struck by the realization that she knows no more of her client now than she did after the first session. On thinking about this problem she realizes that it may be the very feeling of comfort and understanding that she appears to enjoy with this client that is blocking progress. It becomes clear to her that she will need to pay attention to the manner in which her client presents herself and to address this if she is to give the needy part of this woman the chance of coming into the room.

Needless to say the counsellor's withdrawal from this collusive arrangement provokes some rather more basic expressions of resistance in the form of lateness and silence before it is possible to engage the client more fully in the counselling.

---

**Key point**

The client will seek to defend himself by subverting the counselling. The counsellor needs to avoid being drawn into cosy, comfortable relationships.

---

# III

## Developments in Understanding and Working with the Transference

# 13 Allow yourself to become available for use in your client's inner world

Psychodynamic counselling assumes the importance of the client's inner world (Winnicott, 1953). When a client enters a relationship with the counsellor he does so at the level of his deepest need. The quality of his inner world, the nature of his internal objects, will underpin the quality and nature of his relationship to the counsellor. All this will be focused in the transference but none of it may be understood without the capacity of the counsellor to make herself available for use by the client.

As we discussed above, the counsellor provides the setting within which the counselling relationship takes place. A principal element in that setting will be the counsellor herself. Through the maintenance of the setting and the cultivation of her stance she becomes available for the client to use. In a sense she offers herself for usage in the hope that the client will be able to make use of her to communicate what he needs to say about the nature of his inner world. In the previous point we considered how the client and the counsellor can cooperate to subvert the therapeutic aim. Here we turn our attention to the way in which the counselling couple come together to permit the disclosure of the client's unconscious.

In submitting herself to this kind of object usage the counsellor recognizes that the psychodynamic counselling relationship requires the meeting of the counsellor with the client at unconscious levels. She therefore accepts that she is herself destined to become an element in the client's discourse and that without her availability and cooperation he would be unable to articulate his deepest needs. The counsellor needs more than a mere theoretical appreciation of the concept of transference if she is to try to understand her client's inner world. She needs to experience herself as being used within that inner world.

This kind of usage happens at a primitive and unconscious level and depends on such mechanisms as projective and introjective identification. The counsellor may begin to experience herself as taken over by certain kinds of feeling or experience in relation to a particular client. It thus becomes possible for her to experience directly within herself something which belongs to the client and for which he may as yet have no words. For the time being she too may have no words for this experience and she may need to suffer it for quite some while before it becomes possible to talk to the client about it. In this sense the client's capacity to talk about his inner world depends on the availability of the counsellor to be used in this way and to tolerate the confusion and discomfort this may involve.

This kind of availability on the part of the counsellor is related to her capacity for splitting. We may think of the counsellor as having a participating bit and an observing bit within herself. By participating fully in the counselling relationship she opens herself to the full impact of the unconscious communications of her client and at times may be deeply affected by them. Thanks to the observing bit of herself she remains sufficiently in touch with her role as counsellor to be able to reflect on what is happening not only between herself and the client but also within herself. Out of her reflection which, it must not be forgotten, will be supported and developed in supervision, she begins to attach meaning to her clients' attempts at communication. Having allowed herself to become identified with his inner world state through being available for use in the transference, she first struggles within herself to make sense of what she is feeling before trying to talk to the client about those bits of his own experience that he has placed within her.

It will perhaps be clear that in order to combine effectively with the client in this way, the counsellor will need to be able to maintain the detachment of her therapeutic stance. Where the counsellor burdens her stance with too much feeling, too much wanting, she effectively renders herself less available for use by the client. As the client makes use of his counsellor to begin to address the deepest areas of his inner world, there will be quite enough feeling and wanting in the room. Unless the counsellor is able to hold her own emotional needs in reserve, there will be a failure of holding and the client will remain unable to enter a meaningful dialogue. This need for what we might call emotional abstinence on the part of the counsellor will clearly place her under considerable stress at times. It is partly for this reason that those who undertake to become psychodynamic counsellors should themselves have the opportunity for considerable experience as a client in a psychodynamic relationship. Without this safeguard, there is always the danger that far from allowing herself to become available for use by the client, the counsellor begins to abuse him by evacuating unwanted bits of herself into him (Bion, 1962).

The psychodynamic container implies the interplay and some-times the fusing of the inner worlds of the counselling couple. However, through her maintenance of the setting and her own role in it, the counsellor also brings the capacity for observing and reflecting on their interactions and it is this that allows her to become helpful to her client.

## Case example

A woman counsellor brings a male client to supervision. He has come into counselling in connection with a course he has started and finds it difficult to think of himself as a client. In making her presentation the counsellor apologizes for the incompleteness of her notes, remarking that some task had prevented her from recording the session in the normal manner. She presents the session, which had contained much in the way of a report of the client's week, in an episodic manner. The length of her notes suggests she has remembered much of the session, though from time to time she needs to reassure herself about the sequence of events. On finishing her report the counsellor acknowledges that she is feeling anxious about this man though she cannot really understand why. She feels she has lost her usual grasp of the flow of the session and is uncertain about what the client may have been trying to say to her. The supervisor suggests that she may get some indication about his unconscious communication by consulting her own responses to the impact of the session. In doing this the counsellor is able to see that her most acute sense is of confusion and uncertainty, as if she were losing her way. From this she was able to consider that her client, through his use of her in the transference, may be letting her know how disoriented he feels whenever he has to depend on someone else. In the next session she takes the opportunity to address his feelings of confusion and the client responds with a sense of relief at having been, as it were, located.

---

**Key point**

In psychodynamic counselling the client depends on the coun-sellor's ability to interact at conscious and unconscious levels. He cannot completely articulate his needs without being able to make use of the mediation of the counsellor.

# 14  Identify and work with the client's focus of transference

It is well understood that the client in psychodynamic counselling will transfer on to the counsellor feelings, expectations and so on which have their origins in earlier relationships (Malan, 1979). So well is this understood that it can be very tempting for the counsellor to frame most of her remarks along the lines of 'I wonder if this is how you feel about me?' Fundamentally, I think the problem with this kind of remark is that it misses the point about transference, in that primarily it invites the client to focus on the counsellor. While it does happen, with some clients, that the focus of their transference is directly on the person of the counsellor, very often it is not. It is important, therefore, to attend to the client's own directions about transference and to avoid distracting him by attempting to place yourself at the centre of his thoughts. Too much insistence on the centrality of the counsellor in the client's transference references may draw some clients into a compliant attempt to do what they are told.

The point about transference is that it is not about me the counsellor, but about the way in which the counsellor is experienced in terms of the client's inner world. There may be strong transference indications in the client's discourse from the very first session but it is comparatively unusual for a client to be ready to make the link in bald terms. The counsellor needs to take her time and, as it were, gather the transference (Meltzer, 1967) before inviting the client to consider that she is the centre of all his preoccupations. Some clients will experience the attempt to place the counsellor at the centre of his discourse as provocative and alienating, others will see it as seductive and may respond accordingly.

It is important, therefore, in trying to work with the transference, to take your time to reflect on what you may be being drawn into. In the previous point we considered the way in which the client may need to make use of the counsellor to speak about his inner world. Before addressing the transference, the counsellor will need to consider to what end does she become the object of transference. If we remember that it is primarily for the sake of communication, it will help us to see that the transference dynamic in the counselling is an opportunity for the counsellor to make links between early and current life situations and what is going on in the room. Thus the counsellor is the object of transference not in her own right but as a reflecting element in the client's discourse. If she can remember this the counsellor will avoid subverting the relationship and will be able to attend to the client's own focus of transference and to the way in which she is implicated in it.

When attempting to interpret the transference, the counsellor needs to avoid concentrating the dynamic between herself and the client. There needs to be a reference to a third element, which is likely to be the origin of the contents of the transference (Malan, 1979). For this reason asking the client 'I wonder if that's how you feel about me?' leaves out the vital link with the other significant parts of their experience. The counsellor needs herself to understand the way in which her client's transference draws her into association with other parts of the client's life, both in terms of his current relationships and his earlier experiences. Without this linking between all the significant bits of the client's inner world, the psychodynamic dialogue remains incomplete and the client is left alone with his experience, as unable to achieve resolution in the counselling as he has been in other parts of his life.

Through the gathering of the transference and the making of links between the counselling and other parts of the client's experience, the counsellor is establishing the counselling as a container within which meaningful dialogue may be accomplished. The really important communication may need to take place not between the client and the counsellor but between different bits of the client via the counselling relationship. The counsellor, therefore, needs to hold herself ready ever to be the recipient of the client's discourse but also as an element within it through the agency of the transference. By taking her time to identify the client's own focus of transference and working with that, she will facilitate his attempts to disclose himself to her.

## Case example

A woman who had spent her early years with her parents abroad came into counselling with a male counsellor because of conflict in her relationships. She attended regularly, though not always punctually, and filled her sessions with material about current goings on in her life. She had been sent back to school in England as a young child while the parents remained abroad and as an adult she expressed a sense of not really belonging anywhere. Her counsellor found her an interesting and pleasant woman to work with but often found himself feeling lost in her material. However, any attempt he made to interpret her late arrivals or meandering discourse in terms of resistance or anger she might be expressing towards him in the transference, would be rejected. Indeed she seemed to want to make it clear that his efforts to link what she said and did to her possible feelings about him, whether or not in relation to other people in her life, produced no sense of recognition in her at all.

Initially the counsellor felt blocked by her denials, as if her refusal to acknowledge him as the focus of her transference rendered him powerless to work with her. As he continued to listen to her discourse, however, it became apparent that she repeatedly got herself into what might be called transference relationships with other people and his interpretations in connection with these situations were readily accepted. As the counselling progressed, the counsellor came to realize that his earlier attempts to locate himself explicitly in the transference drama interfered with her need to preserve him from her feelings of disappointment and rage and maintain him as a participant in her dialogue and as a witness in her struggles with others who, like her parents, she felt were unwilling to give her a hearing. By abandoning his earlier concern to identify himself as the recipient of transference, the counsellor found the space to identify the client's own focus of transference which allowed her to show him the way in which she needed to make use of him.

---

### Key point

Avoid mechanistic equations when working with transference. Be prepared to let the client take his own time to allow the transference to focus between you, and avoid making yourself an intrusive element in his discourse.

# 15 Identify and address resistance to the counselling

It will be helpful to turn our attention to the issue of resistance at this point, since the focus of the transference is also likely to be the focus for resistance. Resistance is that activity of the client which expresses his most acute need to defend himself in that area of his experience where he feels most vulnerable. Within the counselling relationship it becomes a primary task to identify and work with the resistance before it is really possible to address other issues (Lambert, 1981).

In itself resistance is not that difficult to identity: it is withdrawal of the client from cooperation in the endeavour of counselling to deal with his problems. It may be expressed in the sparseness of material, the inability to think of anything, the superficiality or the density of the content. It may be expressed in the forgetting of things or in the refusal to allow things to add up to anything. It may be signalled by the frequent intrusion of the outer world or a tendency to arrive late. Sometimes the client will make his resistance absolutely clear and not come at all. In these ways and in many others the client shows the counsellor the difficulty he experiences in allowing there to be a fruitful intercourse between them.

This refusal to meet is itself a stressful activity which makes considerable demands on the counsellor's ability to stay with the client. However, resistance does not necessarily represent the wish of the client to end the counselling but rather his need to protect himself from the reality of the relationship that it involves. The counsellor must demonstrate considerable patience in dealing with the resistance and will need to address the anxiety that it covers if she is going to enable the client to abandon his resistance and proceed.

Entry into the counselling relationship implies taking risks. This is so for both parties but especially so for the client who must trust the counsellor with his deepest areas of vulnerability and need. Beyond the achievement of the therapeutic alliance, there has to be the greater achievement of trust at the deepest level.

Until this is established the counselling couple relate to each other at a formal distance and go no further.

In dealing with resistance the counsellor needs to remember that the treatment she receives from the client may provoke in her responses that represent a resistance of her own (Lambert, 1981). Because the client engages with the counsellor at primitive unconscious levels, his behaviour may trigger unconscious and primitive responses in return. It is for this reason that it is important for the counsellor to attend to the client's impact on her and to identify when she has become the object of his resistance. At the point that she has done this, she then needs to turn her attention to the anxiety against which the client is defending. Until the client's anxiety at the deepest levels has been recognized and addressed he will not be able to abandon his resistance and return to his role in the therapeutic alliance.

Dealing with resistance does require considerable effort on the part of the counsellor since the client has withdrawn his co-operation and her efforts to address his anxiety run in the face of his resistance. It is important, therefore, that she avoids sounding accusatory or blaming as this will serve only to drive the client further into his resistance. She will address resistance, therefore, not to tell the client that he is resisting but to allow him the opportunity to address that which makes him anxious.

### Case example

A woman came into counselling with a female counsellor because of a general feeling of stress in her life which manifested itself in various aches and pains in her limbs and in a persistent feeling of tiredness. She began her counselling with a fluent enough account of herself, describing her early life and family history and her current relationships. She presented her material in a spirit of wanting to be helpful to the counsellor but with a general sense of not knowing whether or not something might have a meaning. It became clear that her marriage had not been easy for her and that she had had to manage the strains of childbirth and motherhood without any direct support from her husband or from her own family. Her children were now growing up and over recent years her husband had become involved with other women. Her counsellor reported an impression of a woman embattled and isolated in her struggle to maintain her marriage and family intact.

As the counselling got under way the counsellor noted that the client maintained quite a high degree of formality in the way she conducted herself and she had little sense of the client beginning to relate to her more as a person. Session by session the client seemed to have quite a lot to say but it soon became clear that her primary need was to be able to relate what had happened to her during the week and how she had dealt with it. From time to time the counsellor was able to offer some remark which appeared to clarify things but nothing she said was allowed to refer to the client herself. As time went on the counsellor realized that she was beginning to resent the use the client was making of her, feeling that she was required to listen about everybody else's failures on the one hand and the client's righteous isolation on the other. Her feelings of resentment signalled to her that it was necessary to try to address the client's resistance more directly.

She began by offering the observation that the client seemed most comfortable when she was talking about her day-to-day dealings with others but that it seemed difficult for her to talk about her own deeper feelings or to allow the counsellor any glimpse of what might be going on inside her. In spite of her complaints about the lack of support from others, it seemed that it might be quite frightening for her to think of letting the counsellor into her isolation. The response of the client was quite specific. She could not imagine what else she could possibly talk about. What went on inside her was certainly not for discussion, it was, she considered, private. The counsellor met this response by trying to explore with the client the idea that her symptoms suggested that it might be necessary to confront what was going on inside her, that it could be said that their very purpose was to invite her to pay attention to herself at that level. She recognized from all the client had told her how difficult she might find it to believe that anyone else could be trusted to help her and that her need to fill the time talking about external events served to mask her anxiety about trusting the counsellor. The client received these remarks as interesting and said she would think about them before the next session.

The following day she telephoned to break off the counselling. In this case the client's resistance to engaging herself in the counselling was so acute that the attempt to confront it provoked the ending of the relationship. While this may be unfortunate it is on balance better than prolonging a situation in which resistance prevents any real counselling happening at all.

---

**Key point**

The client needs to experience his counsellor demonstrating her capacity to understand and respect his deepest anxieties, otherwise he has no choice but to protect himself by resisting the counselling process. The counsellor needs to feel the client's anxiety before she can address his resistance.

---

# 16 Accept and contain the development of negativity in the transference

Recognizing and dealing with resistance is important, as we have seen. It is also important to recognize and to work with negativity in the transference (Sandler et al., 1973). As the counsellor sets out to help her client, somewhere within herself she may nurture the idea that the client may come to love her for her efforts on his behalf. We might expect that such an idea forms at least a part of the inner motivation of the counsellor in choosing to involve herself in this most stressful work. Accepting and working with the negativity, the hatred even, of the client, may mount a considerable challenge to the counsellor's ability to work.

It may be thought that the client who has suffered so much in his life comes into counselling in search of a good positive experience, and clearly at one level that must be true. In psychodynamic counselling, however, I believe he comes primarily in search of an opportunity to reach and deal with those parts of his experience at inner and outer world levels that it has not been possible for him to deal with anywhere else. Paradoxically, therefore, the psychodynamic counsellor may do much of her most positive work in the area of the negative transference. The client experiences relief not because he feels that the counsellor loves him where his mother did not, but because he recognizes that she permits him the reality of his own feelings, whatever they may be, and struggles within herself to find ways of talking about them.

With some clients there seems little difficulty in reaching the negative transference and the problem with them is containing the negative feelings enough to be able to make a space to begin to be able to think about them. With others the development of negative feelings within the counselling relationship gives rise to considerable anxiety in the client who believes that the expression of such feelings will inevitably lead to his rejection. The counsellor who is sufficiently in touch with her own need to be loved and accepted will accept her client's negativity whether directly or indirectly expressed, as a communication in the transference and will seek to address it as such. A counsellor who is not sufficiently in touch with her own needs and areas of negativity will experience the client's negative transference as quite persecutory and may be drawn into retaliatory responses. To avoid this danger the counsellor will need to maintain both the internal and external setting of the counselling relationship – as well as having the opportunity for adequate therapy of her own. In this way she provides herself with a framework within which she may begin to think about what the client is doing to her. It is crucial that the counsellor who is the recipient of a powerful negative transference should support herself by working within the boundaries and setting she has provided. Where she does not her capacity to function as a counsellor will be lost and she may find herself slipping into mutually destructive exchanges. It will be seen that the place of supervision in working with the negative transference is vital as it provides the counsellor with a context in which she may safely ventilate her counter-transference responses without risk of evacuating them directly into the client (Bion, 1962). The psychodynamic function of the counsellor may then be preserved as she finds a way of naming the negativity which has been directed into her and thus reaches a point where she can begin to name it for her client.

In many cases the negative transference may not be overwhelming in its character and may even be avoided entirely if the counsellor seems to want to accommodate the client's demands. By being overly warm in her stance and seemingly flexible in her attitude to time and money, the counsellor may collude with the client in creating a cosy relationship in which the negative can have no place. If the counsellor has not had the chance or been able to deal with her own areas of negativity she may contrive to deprive the client of the opportunity to do so by striving to meet his every demand. The client may understand the cue and resign himself to not being able to reach this area of himself in the counselling either. Working within the boundaries and the setting will normally be enough to provide sufficient frustration to draw the negative transference into accessibility.

### Case example

A woman client with a very poor self-image is referred to a male counsellor because of her longstanding depression. She has had counselling before and is pessimistic about the outcome. However, she is clear about her need for help. In working together the counsellor experiences her as a bright and interesting woman and feels struck by the contrast between the appallingly negative account she gives of herself and the apparent facility she has in her discourse, which she uses to block any attempt he makes to offer a positive intervention. The counsellor finds himself drawn into an almost competitive counter-transference in which he seeks to disprove her claim to be no good at anything by drawing her attention to her admirable and often amusing use of language. Whenever he does this, the client becomes upset and states that she has simply failed to convince him of her worthlessness. Her distress is so evident and genuine that the counsellor realizes he must withdraw from the competition.

The difficulty facing him is to know how to tolerate the terribly depressing feelings which arise in him when confronted by such overwhelming negativity. His first step is to recognize that he had begun to feel rejected by his client's failure to respond to his most caring interpretations and that he had begun to retaliate for her refusal to get better by trying to prove her wrong. Having discovered his own need to protect himself against her depressive negativity, he can begin to consider what purpose it might serve for him to be asked so insistently to recognize her awfulness.

He knew from her history that her brother had been ill during childhood, and that her father had found it impossible to tolerate this weakness in his son. She had experienced herself as being used by her father to compensate for the disappointment of his son by requiring her to become something she was not. As the counsellor struggles with his own wish to make her better than she feels herself to be, he comes to see that her need to be allowed to be worthless represents her only escape from the sadistic function she still feels her father wishes her to fulfil in relation to her ill brother. The function of the negativity in this case is to inoculate her against her father's manipulations and so open the way to an experience of herself as a separate and authentic person.

---

**Key point**

If you try to make everything seem positive for the client you risk denying him the chance of expressing vital elements of his personality. Make good use of your internal and external setting to support you in surviving the client's negativity.

---

# 17 Monitor and assess your client's responses to your interventions and interpretations

Given that the work of psychodynamic counselling is largely to do with understanding unconscious processes, it is necessary to have some way of assessing the impact and effect of what the counsellor says to the client. It will be clear from what has been said so far that the counsellor receives the client's discourse as communication within the transference. In responding to what the client says, therefore, the counsellor will seek to make links between the here and now situation of the counselling relationship, factors in the current life situation outside the counselling relationship and finally issues relating to the client's past (Malan, 1979). The client's response to what the counsellor says to him will offer some indication of the appropriateness of her remarks. If an interpretation is well received and responded to with further information the rapport between the counselling couple may be seen to have deepened. Where an intervention meets with rejection or indifference the rapport can be felt to have lessened and the counsellor's remarks were inappropriately offered, even if they were technically correct. It is the fluctuation in the depth of rapport between the counsellor and the client which offers the best indication of the usefulness and appropriateness of an interpretation. Of course, the counsellor cannot expect to interpret correctly all the time and fortunately it is not necessary for her to do so. What is necessary and very important is that the counsellor should pay attention to the way in which the client receives her remarks and be prepared to be prompted or directed by him. The counsellor may sometimes feel convinced that her interpretation is correct and may wish to pursue this even in the face of her client's denial or refusal to respond. It may be that technically it is correct but if it is rejected by the client then it must be considered wrong either at the time that it is given or in the way in which it is given. Where the counsellor becomes attached to her understanding and wishes to persuade the client of her view she has fallen into the error of listening to herself rather than to the client. In order to get the counselling back on track she will have to abandon her certainty and be prepared to follow the client's cues (Casement, 1985).

It may be helpful to remember that the reason the client is here at all is because of his need to defend himself against some terrible anxiety associated with a deeply hidden impulse or feeling. The counsellor's interpretative activity is designed to put the client in touch with what is unconscious within him. It is, therefore, potentially a risky activity for the client since as well as offering him understanding it threatens to erode his defences and so heighten his anxiety. Where the counsellor fails to attend to this risk she forces the client more deeply behind his defences and away from understanding. Thus when the counsellor finds that her best efforts at interpretation are met with silence or rejection she needs to consider that she may have provoked defensive activity and that she will need to address this before attempting to return to her theme.

The aim of the psychodynamic counsellor is to offer the client an experience of a relationship in which he is uniquely offered attention and presence no matter what he does. He may well do a number of things which will make it difficult for the counsellor to offer him either, however, if he experiences himself as safely and adequately held, he will be able to meet the interpretations that are offered. In such a situation he will demonstrate the acceptability of the interpretation by a deepening of rapport.

It should be remembered that not every remark made by the counsellor needs to be thought of as an interpretation. Winnicott spoke of interpreting to show the limits of his understanding (Winnicott, 1969). Sometimes the counsellor speaks simply to ask for clarification or to signal that she is there. At times a client may need to hear that his counsellor is able to survive him. It may be that what is important for the client is not what is said but the voice that says it, or simply the effort to say something. However, the basic principle remains the same, paying attention to the way in which what is said is received is an important guide for the counsellor in assessing the appropriateness of her interventions.

## Case example

A woman client who had been seriously ill as a child is working with a female counsellor in an agency setting. In the last session, the client had been disturbed on arriving late to find that her counsellor was not sitting in her usual chair but at a desk writing. She had expressed her dismay but also made light of it. In the following session the client arrived with a gift of raspberries from her garden. She had been angry after the last session but had decided to bring the raspberries anyway.

*Client*: The last session was really difficult. I thought you weren't there. Then I wondered about it. I could have decided it was nice to find you writing, why did I feel so angry?

*Counsellor*: I wonder if you felt when you didn't find me where you expected that I had abandoned you?

*Client*: It was more frustration you were doing something else.

*Counsellor*: [*waits for a while*]

*Client*: But then I did also feel panic, and yes, grief.

*Counsellor*: [*clarifying*] There seem to have been a number of different feelings, anxiety that I had disappeared, grief at the sense of loss, and rage that I wasn't where you expected me to be.

*Client*: Yes. But did I make it all happen? I don't know whether something is real or whether I have made it up. My children or the raspberries are real enough but I don't know about other things.

*Counsellor*: [*feeling uncertain about what is being discussed but sensing that it may touch on a problem with boundaries*] I am reminded of what you have told me of your mother's difficulty in tolerating your illness. It's as if you have no experience of your mother helping you to contain your anxieties but getting so upset that you were left in serious doubt as to whether you were making mother ill or she was making you ill.

*Client*: That's right. Please don't say anything else for a while. [*Pause*] I dreamed about my husband last night. He was covered in red blotches. They were disgusting. It makes me think about the raspberries, even they seem disgusting now.

*Counsellor*: You said earlier that you thought the raspberries were real enough. In linking them with the dream perhaps you are letting me know that you recognize they may also have a symbolic reference.

*Client*: I know.

*Counsellor*: In previous sessions we have made the link between red and rage and so perhaps the gift of fruit has two meanings, the first to do with a positive connection between us, your feeding me with the first fruits, and second to do with your anger with me.

*Client*: Yes, I could throw them at you, so you'd be spattered with blotches, like in the dream.

*Counsellor*: [*encouraged by this confirmation*] I feel your dream links back to what happened last time. When you didn't find me where you expected me to be, you weren't sure whether you had destroyed me, hence the need to restore me with the fruits, or if I had abandoned you, thus your wish, disguised in the fruits, to punish me.

In this example we see the counsellor paying attention to the client's responses to her interventions which leads to a satisfactory exploration of the client's internal dilemmas.

---

**Key point**

In psychodynamic counselling communication happens at different levels. The counsellor needs to assess what the client does with her interventions and to be guided by this.

---

# 18   Monitor and attend to the presence of sexuality in the relationship between you and the client

Like any other human relationship psychodynamic counselling is a context where sexuality and sexual material may make themselves felt. Being comfortable with sexual matters and with your own sexuality are important aspects of the counsellor's presence in the room. While our understanding of transference and, of course, counter-transference leads us to expect the appearance of sexual material in the client's discourse, we may be taken off guard when it actually appears.

It is important I believe to distinguish between sexual references in the material which are clearly embedded in the infantile transference and relate to early phases of the client's development and those which reflect more directly on the adult personality of the client. In the former case it is important for the counsellor to receive these references in the context of the client's regression and to address them accordingly. In the latter case it is more a question of managing the boundaries of the relationship without inflicting injury to the dignity of the client.

Similarly, the counsellor needs to monitor her own responses in relation to the client so as to be aware of the appearance of any sexual feelings or fantasies. As with any other kind of feeling the counsellor may discover within herself in relation to the client, she needs to accept the presence of sexual feelings or ideas and consider in what way they may be relevant to the unfolding of the counselling relationship. Again, as with other emotions that may register in the counsellor, it is not usually appropriate to speak directly to the client about these. It is, however, right that she should dialogue with herself about them and not push them out of mind as being out of place or embarrassing. If we remember that whatever emerges within the container of the transference counter-transference dynamic needs to be considered as a potential communication in the therapeutic discourse, it may become easier to confront the sexual material.

Bringing such material into supervision can often seem something of an ordeal for the counsellor, especially where she is anxious to be perceived as getting it right. It should be remembered, however, that it is the supervisor's function not to judge but to facilitate the counsellor's understanding of the whole counselling relationship. A capacity for sexual responsiveness is normal in human development and is often a goal we might hope to foster in our clients. The ability to recognize the potential for sexual attraction in relation to the client, while not directly expressed, may form an important element in the client's experience of being valued and held in regard by the counsellor. A clear understanding of the ethical requirement to refrain from sexual contact with the client, is usually sufficient to safeguard the boundaries and maintain the therapeutic character of the relationship.

It should also be borne in mind that sexual material or feelings may be used by the client as a way of resisting the therapeutic process (Greenson, 1967). If the client seems to be generating an atmosphere of erotic tension in the room, which he or she may do by dress, behaviour or remarks, it is likely that the intention is to subvert the counselling. The counsellor needs to respond to the level of anxiety which is being masked by the sexual content and avoid getting drawn into the seduction. The counsellor will find it easier to manage this type of transference if she has had an adequate opportunity to resolve her own sexual issues in the safety of a responsible therapeutic relationship. Finally, it may be noted, that the appearance of sexual material or feelings may occur in the client or the counsellor irrespective of whether they are of the opposite or the same sex. Sexual feelings or material arising where the client and the counsellor are of the same sex need to be received and worked with in exactly the same way as applies when the counselling couple are of opposite sex.

### Case example

A young man has been in counselling with a male counsellor for some considerable time. At the outset of the relationship he had appeared very cut off from his feelings and sounded very much like an automaton. His parents were divorced and it seemed he had felt dominated by both of them in different ways. His father in particular was very difficult for him to please. For quite a bit of the counselling relationship his discourse has been about his overriding need to be able to control his life and everything in it. This eventually appeared in the counselling in the form of a sullen and withdrawn retreat into silence, which went on for several weeks.

The stand-off was abruptly and surprisingly broken by the client's sudden announcement that he was thinking about the counsellor's penis. The counsellor said nothing in reply to the client's remark but registered a strong feeling of sexual anxiety within himself. It felt at first as if the client might be wanting something sexual to occur between them. He decided to seek clarification and ask what the thought had been. The client responded that he wanted to touch his penis and then smash it through the window. The counsellor realized that his own fantasy had been both correct and wrong. It appeared that the client wanted to possess whatever the counsellor's penis might signify, and then to destroy it, that is to make him feel its loss. It occurred to the counsellor that his penis might represent a breast to the client. The long silences had expressed a terrible feeling of being cut off and powerless. What had initially appeared as a sexual wish was revealed to be a powerful desire to establish intimate possession of what to the client seemed powerful in the counsellor and then to destroy it. Having allowed himself the space to reflect in this way, the counsellor was able to overcome his own feelings of anxiety and begin to talk to the client about his powerful feelings of envy and rage.

**Key point**

Sexuality in the counselling relationship needs to be understood and managed with the same care and sensitivity as anything else; it may be a vehicle of communication or a means of destructive resistance.

# IV Developments in Understanding and Working with Counter-Transference

# 19 Observe and digest your own responses to client material

Transference and counter-transference were recognized early in the development of the psychoanalytic process. However, it was not originally understood that counter-transference could be useful in the counsellor's understanding of the client. Over the years counter-transference has come to be understood as a key factor in the therapeutic relationship without which the counsellor can have no hope of understanding or helping her client (Laplanche and Pontalis, 1973).

Basically the counsellor needs to recognize two kinds of counter-transference. The first is counter-transference proper which we will consider here. The second is neurotic counter-transference, which has for more to do with the counsellor than with the client and is an indication of inadequate personal therapy. It will often be important to the counsellor to be able to discuss in her own therapy issues that confront her in work with her own clients and this is all to the good. However, there is always a danger without sufficient personal therapy, that the counsellor may import into work with her clients unresolved issues of her own, which if not checked may be destructive.

Having sounded a note of caution about neurotic counter-transference, we may turn our attention to counter-transference proper. If we accept that everything the client says or does may be received as a communication in the transference, we may also consider that anything that comes unbidden into the counsellor's mind may be understood as counter-transference. Just as there is a meeting at the conscious level between the counsellor and the client, so there is a meeting between them at the level of the unconscious. It may therefore happen that the level at which understanding first takes place will also be unconscious and that this will only become available to the counsellor via the agency of her counter-transference.

In practice the counsellor needs to learn to pay attention to her own feelings, impulses, fantasies and so on in response to client material and be prepared to consider that they may be meaningful elements in the overall communication. However, it will not usually be possible or even correct to attempt to speak directly to the client about what is going on inside the counsellor. Where the counter-transference is accurately in tune with the client's inner world, it will still usually require digesting and reformulation before it can be used to address the client.

The point about counter-transference is that it pertains to communication at depth. It still requires interpretation if it is to contribute to understanding at depth. Therefore, the counsellor needs to subject her own counter-transference activity to an interpretative enquiry within herself before she can make use of it to understand her client. The presence of different responses within herself in relation to the client alerts the counsellor to a particular focus for her thinking and understanding. It may be that initially she discovers that she is so affected by a particular client that she is unable to think or to understand anything. The feeling in the counter-transference seems to be one of numbness or confusion. The intensity of this kind of response may be such that it takes the counsellor quite some time to recover contact with an observing bit of herself which may register what is happening and allow her to begin to reflect on it. Once she is able to attend to what is going on inside her, the counsellor may begin to consider her feeling state as itself an element in the client's communication. At this point she recovers for herself the possibility of relating that to what is going on between them. It is important that the counsellor does not simply evacuate the intense feeling into the client in an effort to relieve herself of what may be very difficult to bear. First of all she needs to identify this feeling state within herself and to attempt to treat it there before beginning to speak to the client about it. She does this by trying to contain her own feeling state within the matrix of her understanding. Only when she has done this is she free to use counter-transference as a means of understanding the client.

Not all counter-transference responses will be so intense, and sometimes they may seem so slight that it will be possible to ignore them. For this reason it is important that the counsellor should learn to attend to her own emotional and mental activity while she listens to the client, so as to be able to draw on her unconscious understanding of his material. At times, the counter-transference material, rather like the variations in rapport between the client and the counsellor, will be a guide as to the direction the communication is taking. At other times, the counter-transference will be the communication itself and will require the counsellor's full participation and cooperation if it is ever to be understood.

The problem for the counsellor in being able to make use of her counter-transference responses is that they often take a form which may strike her as inappropriate or perhaps even wrong. It can be distracting, if nothing else, for the counsellor to find that as her client recounts some seemingly innocuous events of his week, that fantasies of say a sexual or violent nature are scudding across her mind. However, if she can bring herself to overcome her reticence about the appropriateness of such fantasies and attend instead to what is going on in them, she may discover that she is tracking a theme that is all too relevant to what her client is saying or doing. If we remember that the unconscious expresses itself indirectly, via metaphor or symbol, we may allow ourselves to censor nothing from our counter-transference material, so long as we then subject it to the same interpretative enquiry we apply to the client's material. The whole thrust of psychodynamic counselling is the exploration of a relationship which looks for meaning. Both the client and the counsellor may experience themselves as at times subject and at times object in this relationship; they must therefore both submit themselves to the investigation of their unconscious.

## Case example

A very experienced woman counsellor begins work with a health care professional who is pursuing her own training in counselling. The client identifies difficulties in sustaining relationships as her greatest problem. She has risen to a role of considerable responsibility at her place of work and supervises junior colleagues. She is an only child and feels she may have been an encumbrance to her parents who sent her away to school at an early age. At the assessment session the counsellor is struck by her client's resemblance to a former supervisor who is prominent in the field and much respected. She takes note of the very professional way in which the client presents herself and of her fluency in the psychodynamic tongue. She also notes that she finds the client likeable and engaging. As the client gives an account of herself, punctuated with analytical comment and interpretation, the counsellor observes herself feeling less relaxed and almost in awe. From time to time memories of uncomfortable sessions with her former supervisor spring to mind and she recalls herself to attention with the realization that she has not heard what the client has been saying. She recognizes the beginnings of feelings of irritation coupled with competitiveness. While she is struggling with these feelings she also observes that the client does not seem altogether sure of herself in spite of her powerful presentation. At times her interpretations seem tentative, as if she might be looking for confirmation of their correctness.

As she attends to the client and her discourse, the counsellor becomes aware that she is developing strong counter-transference responses and recognizes that initially it is important simply to take note of these and not to let them distract her attention. When the session is over the counsellor takes the time to review her responses in relation to what the client was actually saying. She recognizes her identification of the client with her former supervisor as pointing to a still unresolved transference of her own to a powerful parent figure, with whom she also felt competitive. She goes on to note the impact of the client's sophisticated and knowing presentation of herself and reflects that she may be being invited to admire her, thus suggesting the possibility of a narcissistic defence. She recognizes that her own positive feelings in relation to the client may be in response to the client's need to make meaningful contact with her but may also reveal a wish of her own to avoid difficult feelings developing between them. The mixture of tension and awe coupled with irritation and competition alert the counsellor that she is responding to a very complex internal picture in the client. Her observation that the client may be less sure of herself than her presentation would suggest confirms this and helps her to modify the impact of her own feelings of uncertainty.

---

**Key point**

Psychodynamic counselling is very much a two-way process. As counsellor you are as much the object of attention and enquiry as is the client.

---

# 20  Balance your feeling and thinking activities in your practice of counselling

The therapeutic encounter between counsellor and client can be very intense. The people who turn to counsellors for help have usually suffered a great deal and their stories may be very moving. It will not be unusual, therefore, for the counsellor to have strong feeling responses to the client. This is as it should be since it is difficult to imagine how a client may be helped by a counsellor who is not able to resonate with basic human feelings. The feelings we find as counsellors in response to the client are themselves ingredients in the formation of a therapeutic space as they place the counsellor in emotional contact with the client and demonstrate her ability to be present with him.

The capacity to feel with someone as they unfold their story is clearly an important element in the process of psychodynamic counselling. Without accurate empathy as it is called, the client will not feel held and may never feel understood. The counsellor, therefore, needs to feel free to have feeling responses and to attend to them. There may be times when feeling with the client is largely what is called for and any kind of interpretative intervention would be at best unnecessary and at worst intrusive. The counsellor needs to learn that she is not always required to say something and that sometimes her silent but feeling presence is everything that is needed.

Accepting the importance of her own feelings in the therapeutic relationship allows the psychodynamic counsellor to consider their meaning. While it can be important at times to feel but say nothing, it will often be the case that the counsellor's feeling responses require her to think about them. We should never underestimate the reparative work that can be done in a counselling relationship by the reliable provision of a facilitating environment where the counsellor's chief therapeutic activity is that of being there with her feelings in a setting that is consistently held (Winnicott, 1963). However, beyond the provision of a context for being, there will eventually be the need for a context for thinking and this context must also stem from the counsellor. It is important, therefore, that alongside her capacity to feel with the client, the counsellor should develop her ability to think about the impact the client has on her at a feeling level.

The capacity to think about feelings in the therapeutic relationship is akin to the mediating the mother performs in relation to her infant's impact on her (Bion, 1967; Casement, 1985). As the child cries he puts some bit of himself into mother for her urgent attention. If she is able to tolerate his use of her in this way, she feels what he is doing intensely, but she also begins to think about it so that she can offer him a response. Her first thought may not be correct and she will continue to think until he is able to accept what she offers and feels whole again. In a similar way the counsellor seeks to mediate the impact of her client's communication. She identifies the feeling state within herself and through her thinking produces something she can say to him which alleviates his feelings and also allows him to begin to think too. In this way he has the chance of internalizing the capacity to think about things which may eventually enable him to deal with his own anxieties.

The counsellor will often have to struggle very hard to hold on to her own capacity to think about what is happening with a particular client, not least because the client may defend himself against the process of thinking (Bion, 1967). For this reason it is important the counsellor should seek to balance feeling responses with thinking. To ask herself what the feelings are about, who is feeling them and why, provides her with a space within herself where she may continue to function as a counsellor. Without such a space she may experience herself as disappearing within the client's feeling state projected into her. In such a situation she is overwhelmed by her counter-transference and will be unable to function.

### Case example

A trainee talked to her own counsellor about her experience of beginning to work with clients. In particular she referred to a supervision discussion in which a fellow trainee had talked about feeling so overwhelmed by the sadness in his client's life that he had begun crying in the session along with the client. The supervisor had apparently made it clear that this kind of response was not acceptable. The trainee was disturbed by this as she had found herself close to tears with a client of her own and felt unsure whether she would always be able to control her own feeling responses to the client. It seemed especially hard as her placement in a college counselling service meant that most of her clients were of a similar age to her own children. She recognized there were times when she felt like putting her arm round a client or even taking them home for a good meal.

The counsellor responded by exploring with the trainee the extent to which her reality as the mother of young people whom she could no longer care for directly because of their absence at college, might at times intrude on her ability to contain her own anxieties about her children when confronted with clients in a similar situation. The trainee began to realize that her failure to come to terms with the separation from her own children might be interfering with her capacity to work with her clients and that the strength of her feeling responses had more to do with her own needs than with her client's pain. The counsellor accepted that this might be the case but also suggested that her anxiety not to displease her supervisor might persuade her to reject all her feeling responses as unacceptable, whereas what may really have been of concern to the supervisor was the undigested and un-recognized outpouring of feeling. In raising the issue in her own counselling, perhaps the trainee wanted to check out whether her counsellor agreed with the supervisor that having feelings about or in response to clients was unacceptable.

---

**Key point**

In psychodynamic counselling a capacity for empathy needs to be balanced by a capacity for thinking. You cannot function as a counsellor without the capacity to digest the client's material.

## 21 Use supervision, peer groups and personal therapy to work with your counter-transference

We have already considered the importance of the setting for the process of psychodynamic counselling. In the area of counter-transference setting is especially important from the counsellor's point of view. For the counsellor the concept of setting extends beyond the counselling room to supervision, peer groups and personal therapy. The counsellor is fortunately not alone in her encounter with the client and therefore her struggles with counter-transference can find support in two quite distinct contexts. The need to think, as outlined above, can be greatly helped by the process of supervision. By supervision I mean both the formal supervision whether individual or group, provided by the training body, and the less formal but responsible discussion of work with one's peers. (I do not mean the careless discharge of feelings which can take place when the counsellor feels the need to get rid of something without thinking about it.) The other context is, of course, personal therapy where a counsellor may well expect to need to talk about the impact of particular clients on her own inner world.

The counsellor, whether or not still in training, needs to feel that she can make use of her own setting to help her in the work with her clients. Because in psychodynamic counselling the unconscious process involves the counsellor so intimately and deeply in her work, it is both natural and necessary that she should need to talk to someone else about what is happening. Because she wants to do well in her training and perhaps to impress the supervisor, the counsellor may seek to use supervision as an opportunity to demonstrate what she knows. While understandable, this is a pity since the purpose of supervision is not primarily to assess the counsellor, even though that has to be done, but to think about what is happening in the counselling relationship. Supervision externalizes that bit of the counsellor which is trying to think about the client and supports it by bringing a third into the couple relationship (Mander, 1993).

The intensity of the relationship between counsellor and client is such that it may become extremely difficult for the counsellor to retain any space within herself to think about what is going on. Where she recognizes supervision as a context which is supportive of her function as counsellor she will be able to make use of the supervisor to understand what is happening between herself and the client and then what is happening within the client. In supervision she is able to stand apart briefly from the intensity of her interactions with the client and join up with a more objective part of herself as counsellor. This permits her to begin to reflect on her involvement with the client and so to re-establish any part of herself which may have been taken over by him. In this way she is enabled to survive the use her client makes of her as well as preparing herself to meet such use in future sessions. Thus by opening up the couple relationship she has with the client to the observations and reflections of the supervisor she reclaims and supports for herself that aspect of her relationship with the client which seeks to help him.

It has to be acknowledged that I am assuming a good enough supervisor for the counsellor to work with (Winnicott, 1953). As in any relationship, there will be conscious and unconscious dynamics at play which may interfere with the supervision as a benign and supportive influence on the counsellor's work. It is for supervisors to pay attention to their part in the dynamics of the supervisory relationship. The counsellor facing difficulties in her work with a client or in handling the relationship with a supervisor, has the further context of her personal therapy in which to find help.

Intense transference counter-transference involvements, whether with client or supervisor, are likely to confront the counsellor at some point with the need to work on these problems in her own therapy. In a sense this is both a personal need and a training need. Personally, the setting of her own therapy permits the further resolution of some aspect of her own object-relating constellated by her work. This resolution in her own inner world allows the counsellor to differentiate between what belongs to her and what to the client and so frees her to work with what he brings.

It is important that the counsellor should not deprive herself of the help that is available to her in her encounter with the client. Psychodynamic counselling can be a very lonely activity, with the counsellor believing that she is required to hold everything herself. She may come to believe that supervision is about judgement and that personal therapy has nothing to do with her own case work. If she does she is forced into an isolation which is good neither for her nor for her client. If she can come to see that supervision and therapy are for her to make use of, she will find her ability to work with her clients enhanced.

### Case example

A trainee counsellor emerges from a session with one of her clients looking drawn and tired. In the staff room she confides in her colleagues that she is feeling particularly dispirited by her apparent failure to get anywhere with her client who seems unwilling to accept any of her interventions. She is beginning to feel that perhaps it was a mistake to think she could do this work and maybe she should consider withdrawing from the course. Her peers offer their sympathy and support and one suggests she might be feeling what the client feels. In her own therapy later in the day she talks about her misgivings about whether she is doing the right thing and that she is feeling useless and helpless. She talks at some length about her frustrations in being unable to get through to her client. Her therapist offers an interpretation about other relationships she has had where she has also felt unable to get through and suggests that her own earlier experiences may be making it difficult for her to tolerate her client's apparent refusal to let her in, just as she has also felt at times that her therapist was keeping her out.

In further discussion of her feelings it becomes apparent that the counsellor has avoided bringing her concerns about this client to her supervisor and her therapist encourages her to do so. At her next supervision session she presents the client and is surprised to find the supervisor responding sympathetically to her difficulties. She begins to see that her problems in working with this client may not be a reflection of her competence as a counsellor, but rather that her self-doubt and despondency were in tune with the client's hidden feelings of emptiness.

By emerging from the isolation she had been falling into in her work with this client, by discussing her work in therapy and supervision, the counsellor was enabled to recognize aspects of her own terrible feelings as responses in the counter-transference.

---

**Key point**

Do not allow yourself to get cut off from the support for your work that is available. Managing counter-transference often requires you actively to discuss your responses in appropriate contexts.

---

## 22 Allow for the interference of your own unresolved conflicts in the process of the counselling

The genius of the psychodynamic approach to counselling is the extent to which it makes use of the client's relationship with the counsellor as the primary therapeutic agent. It follows, therefore, that the personality of the counsellor is a key factor in the counselling process. Hence the primary importance of personal therapy in the development of the psychodynamic counsellor. In a sense it is a curious thing that the counsellor sets out to do, since she knows that to work effectively with any client she must be prepared to expose herself to the reality of his inner world. It is as if the counsellor knowingly allows herself to be infected by the client in order that she may accurately recognize the reality of his inner world situation, treat it within herself and then attempt to treat it in him (Bollas, 1987). What, we may well ask, is in it for the counsellor? Apart from any status she may acquire by becoming a counsellor, we may also consider that she deals with some of her own deepest anxieties by becoming someone who can resolve problems, an expert if you will. It will be apparent that we are in the area of psychological functioning to do with splitting (Guggenbühl-Craig, 1971). Clients need help, counsellors give it; clients are empty, counsellors are full and so on. These kinds of splits can be very persuasive and some clients will collude with their counsellor in their maintenance. It is of course necessary that the counsellor in training should begin to develop confidence in herself and her ability to do the work. However, she needs also to remain open to the way in which areas of her own inner world may remain in conflict and may become disruptive to her counselling.

The need to appear to know what you are doing in the eyes of both the client and the training organization may make it very difficult for the counsellor to own and work with her own areas of conflict. Anxiety about being found wanting may encourage the counsellor to develop a kind of false self (Winnicott, 1960) in regard to her work, conforming with what is thought to be required and affecting a fluency in discussion which is only superficial. Such adaptations may bolster sagging confidence but they tend to interfere with the counsellor's actual ability to work effectively with her clients.

It is for this reason that there is usually such a strict separation observed between training and personal therapy. The counsellor's own therapy needs to be experienced as being genuinely separate from the critical assessments of the training body so that she may freely confront her own inner world conflicts in whatever way she can. Where the counsellor feels secure enough to work with her true self she will from time to time come up against issues of the client's which so overlap with her own issues that she is temporarily unable to work with them. If she recognizes this is what is happening she will be able to bring these issues to her own therapy and work with them there. Having had the opportunity to work through what belongs to her she will then be free to help the client go further with his conflicts. If she is not free to recognize what is happening then her own unresolved conflicts will interfere with her ability to help the client. A problem arises for the counsellor if she feels the need to present a knowing and expert self to her clients and trainers.

### Case example

A trainee counsellor begins work with a female client who works in a women's hostel. She has a positive feeling for this client as she supports the kind of work she is doing. Her client has come for counselling because of difficulties in her relationship with her mother and problems in finding a partner for herself. The trainee is surprised to discover that her early good feelings for the client give way before long to less positive and comfortable feelings. She begins to experience her client as droning on, endlessly inviting her to collude in a woefully pessimistic view of life from which there can be no respite. Her attempts to point to positive areas in the client's experience and the value of her work are overwhelmed by the client's insistence on the meaninglessness of everything. As the work proceeds with this client the counsellor finds herself feeling more and more despondent. At the same time the client attends her sessions with regularity and even implies that they may be useful to her.

Not long after starting to work with this client the counsellor begins to have a series of dreams in which she is required to stand at the kitchen sink before endless piles of dirty, greasy plates. No matter how hard she works the washing up never goes away. Initially she pays little attention to these dreams until one day she recognizes that the despondency she feels with her client is very similar to the way in which she feels in her dreams. Having made this link she is then able to see the relevance of the very domestic imagery of the dream in referring to the experience of women and more specifically to her experience of her own mother whom she thought of as a martyr to drudgery. It then becomes clear to her that she has failed to recognize her anger with her mother for the unremitting monotony of her complaints about the prison of drudgery while seeming to expect her daughter to share her confinement. Having recognized these feelings the counsellor finds it is not difficult to see that her own unresolved conflict with her mother has begun to make it unbearable for her to be with her client. Having recognized these conflicts within herself she is now able to understand the dilemma facing her client, whose conscious dedication to the cause of women has left her no outlet for her rage against her own mother.

---

### Key point

In psychodynamic counselling the personality of the counsellor is intricately involved in the therapeutic process. Things that belong to the counsellor will inevitably get stirred up by the client and will require attention.

23  Attend to the impact of your client's discourse as well as to the content

One of the main anxieties facing the new counsellor in training is how will she ever remember all that the client says to her in the course of a session. This can seem particularly daunting when she is faced with the need to record a session in detail for the purposes of supervision. Cursory notes made on the main themes of the session recorded immediately at its end are often found to be enough to unlock the detail of what is said for later recall. With experience the counsellor learns to trust her capacity to hold what has been said and to record it in her notes.

However, even a counsellor who has learned to be less anxious about writing up the notes, may find that at times she is unable to recall much of the detail of a session. It may seem that a lot was said, or maybe that very little was said, but that it is peculiarly difficult to retain any of it. This can be very disconcerting, as if in spite of her best efforts to attend to the client, the counsellor has allowed him to disappear. When it seems difficult to track what the client may be saying, it may be helpful to focus attention not so much on his words but on their impact (Casement, 1985). The client always comes to tell us something, but he may not be able to do so directly in words. The counsellor may need the courage to allow the words to float over her while she permits her own attention to focus on the effect of the client's discourse within her. By attending to what she is experiencing and feeling she opens herself to receive the important communication. If on the contrary she struggles to remain with the surface content of what he is saying, she may find that she understands nothing at all.

Psychodynamic counselling assumes the importance of unconscious communications and the counsellor, therefore, needs to develop her capacity to listen beneath the surface. She does this primarily by paying attention to her own counter-transference. At the beginning of her training, a major difficulty for the counsellor is in learning how to trust and make use of her own counter-transference responses. To do so requires a shift from our more accustomed way of knowing about things through rational and cognitive processes to a more irrational and intuitive way, linked with feelings and fantasy. Learning to accept the validity of feelings and ideas occurring within herself as a basis for knowing about and understanding the client, is a basic task for the counsellor.

There will be times when there is no particular problem in following what is being said or in retaining it. At the same time the counsellor will find herself aware of feelings which do not seem to be in accord with what is being said. Again it is important that the counsellor should feel able to make use of her counter-transference responses and address the discrepancy between content and impact. By doing this the counsellor demonstrates to the client her willingness to listen at deeper levels and to think about his conflicts. The client brings himself to the counselling relationship as best he can and in the hope that he will find an available presence in the person of the counsellor. In addition to her theoretical understanding and her ability to provide and maintain the setting, the counsellor brings to the relationship her ability and readiness to resonate emotionally with the client. At times she will be called upon to do this by registering massive impact by the client on her feeling states. Like the mother attending to the crying of her infant, she must pay attention to this impact if she is to discover what her client is really trying to say.

### Case example

A male counsellor is working with a young female client who has difficulty in making relationships with men, which she relates to the intrusive nature of her relationship with her father. She is established in counselling and her material often ranges over a wide number of themes. In one session the client begins talking about problems she has recently been experiencing with a colleague at work whom she feels is over-solicitous for her health. The counsellor discovers that he finds it difficult to pay attention to what she is saying and is surprised to find an image from a television programme he has recently seen returning to his mind. The image is of a couple shopping together and disappearing into a changing cubicle where they make love. He is distracted by this image and attempts to dismiss it and to return his attention more properly to his client. However, he discovers that the imagery is insistent and, therefore, decides not to resist it. As he considers what this might be about he remembers that the antics of the couple are apparent to other shoppers and in particular a middle-aged woman, who is obviously disapproving. He begins to consider that his fantasy might have a bearing on what his client is trying to say to him. He offers an interpretation:

*Counsellor*: It occurs to me that what you have been telling me about your over-solicitous colleague may link at some level with how you feel about the bit of me that may be concerned to look after you.

*Client*: Perhaps. I don't need looking after all the time. I don't want other people sticking their noses in my business.

*Counsellor*: It seems you want to be free to do what you want without critical intrusion but that it is not always easy for you to maintain your own privacy.

*Client*: There's always someone ready to disapprove.

*Counsellor*: [*drawing on his fantasy*] I have been thinking that your problems with your colleague refer to your earlier difficulties with your father. It seems that your father's intrusiveness resonated at some level with your own wish to be intimate with him, but that by seeming to press himself on you he stirred up anxiety caused by the feelings of guilt you had about pushing your mother out. In a similar way I think you link your colleague with what you experience as my wish to press my concern on you, which stirs up anxiety about mother's disapproval.

*Client*: I never knew what mum was thinking but I often felt uncomfortable when she was around.

By attending to his fantasy the counsellor finds his way deeper into the client's concerns and thus allows himself to be directed by her unconsciously to what matters.

---

**Key point**

It is quite easy to get lost in the client's discourse but you can often find your way by attending to what you register within yourself, whether feeling, mood or fantasy.

---

# 24   Be prepared to get it wrong and to build on that

Perhaps the last thing that the counsellor in training expects to be of help to her client is that she should make a mistake and get something wrong. However, it is precisely just such a situation, acknowledged and well handled by the counsellor, that can bring about progress in the work (Casement, 1985). Where a counsellor is experienced by the client as being perfect and all-knowing, she may also be experienced as being of no use to him.

The client who comes into psychodynamic counselling does so in search of a good enough fit with the counsellor. Of course he needs her to understand him and to get things right but he also needs her to address his anxieties about the nature of his internal objects. If the counsellor never makes a mistake she also never allows an opportunity for acknowledging her failure and for making amends. The client may therefore experience her as a correct but cold object with whom he can make no meaningful contact.

We may imagine the situation in which the infant receives all that he needs at a functional level, there is holding of a kind, there is food, there is survival and continuity and yet mother never quite becomes meaningful to him as a person. When such a person becomes a client he may go a long way with the counsellor doing her best work, without it really getting through to him. The counsellor may find herself feeling that everything is going well but that nothing is really happening. It may only be when the counsellor finds herself making a mistake and getting something wrong that the opportunity for change arises.

Such is the power of the idea that counsellors are there to help their clients that it can be extremely difficult for the counsellor to allow herself to deal with having made a mistake in a constructive way. She may feel bad that she has let the client down, or perhaps angry that she has let herself down. She may feel ashamed, that her supervisor or peers will think ill of her, that the training body will decide she is unfit to be a counsellor. The scope for persecutory responses to discovering she has made a mistake or got something wrong is so great that it can often be difficult for the counsellor to find any space within herself to think about what has happened as itself being meaningful within the relationship with the client. Naturally, it can happen that events in the external world in the counsellor's own life can impinge on her counselling and cause her to get things wrong. However, even in this situation, so long as the counsellor is able to work constructively with what has occurred, it may be possible for the error to contribute to the progress of the counselling. It is only where the counsellor fails to recognize the source of the disturbance or to appreciate the likely impact of its impingement on the client that damage may be done. Usually, however, the reason the counsellor makes a mistake will not be attributable solely to her but will find its explanation within the transference counter-transference dynamic. The client himself will provide the occasion for the mistake because he needs to experience the counsellor as able to acknowledge her failing and her willingness to work with it.

Where the counsellor is able to allow herself to get things wrong, she may paradoxically learn how to get something right. Where the client is unconsciously prompting the counsellor to make a mistake, he is communicating to her at the deepest level, and if she is able to acknowledge the mistake and seek to understand it, she allows herself to be used by him in precisely the way that he needs.

The important point is that the counsellor should develop enough freedom in relation to her work to be able to accept that she will get things wrong and that sometimes she may need to get something wrong if the client is to make real contact. If she is able to moderate the injury to her narcissism she may discover that her capacity to make mistakes can be of positive value to the client without which he would be unable to leave his experience of correct but empty relating.

The order of the mistake may vary considerably. Sometimes the counsellor manages to forget the client altogether and misses a session. This would clearly be an extreme case likely to deliver the counsellor a considerable jolt. There is in other words something so painfully wrong with this situation that it is crying out for the counsellor's considered attention. Perhaps the client is saying something like, 'It's as if we are not meeting at all!' A counsellor who does such a thing is likely to feel terrible. So long as she is not swamped by them, these terrible feelings may be useful to her in tuning in to how terrible it feels for the client. When she begins to use her feelings to understand him in this way she becomes useful to him and the work may proceed. It is more usual that the nature of the mistake is much less dramatic in kind. Perhaps the counsellor forgets something that has been told her, or remembers something incorrectly. The danger in this situation is that the client and the counsellor merely clarify what is wrong without any attention being paid to the fact that a mistake has been made. In this case it is possible that small mistakes will continue to be made until the counsellor is able to turn her attention to what is happening.

## Case example

A male counsellor is working with a woman who has referred herself for help with her depression. She had been ill as a child, spending time away from her family in hospital. As an adult she became seriously depressed and at one point had to spend a period of time in hospital. At the time of her referral she was not particularly depressed and it became apparent that she had other reasons for coming into counselling. She had previously been in counselling with a woman, which had been successful, but she now sought the opportunity to work with a man.

Her sessions are characterized by much rich material which is stimulating and interesting but sometimes difficult for the counsellor to contain. In the initial phase of the work she brings a very positive, almost idealized transference. She is clearly appreciative of the counsellor's attention and admiring of his interventions. The counsellor finds her an interesting and rewarding client to work with but is aware that at times he may be in danger of becoming lost in the abundance of the material. Everything seems to be going well until one session in which the client discovers that her counsellor has apparently forgotten some detail she had given him the previous week. She is angry and seemingly incredulous at this lapse, wondering how she can possibly trust a counsellor who forgets what he has been told. Initially the counsellor feels hurt and defensive in response to her criticisms, feeling that she is ready to rubbish the whole coun-selling relationship over a quite minor matter. He then allows himself to consider that this forgetting may have some purpose in relation to their work together. He realizes that his mistake has occasioned the first expression of negative feeling in their relationship but that this has plunged immediately into deep areas of anxiety about trust and reliability. In subsequent sessions the client seems to return to her former good feelings until a similar mistake occurs with similar consequences. Over a long period of time it emerges that the rhythm of the work is to be punctuated by these mistakes and that, very gradually, the client uses them to replace her idealization of the counsellor with a more ambivalent but realistic regard.

---

**Key point**

The client needs to make authentic contact with the counsellor. Sometimes the only way he can do this is by unconsciously forcing an error which requires both client and counsellor to focus on its meaning.

---

# V Developments in Working with the Whole Counselling Relationship

# 25   Respect and interpret your client's defences

As you begin working with clients you will soon discover that the very person who is asking for help will apparently withdraw their cooperation. Resistance, as it is called, is a form of defence and therefore its purpose is to protect the client. Understanding the client's need to defend himself is absolutely basic, and without it the counselling relationship is likely to founder on the rocks of resistance (Lambert, 1982).

The need for defence potentially presents the counselling couple with something of an impasse, since it is likely that defences will have to come down if progress is to be made and yet protecting himself against pain is going to be important to the client. He will understand that you will want to breach his defences in order to be of help to him but he will also experience you in the transference as a source of anxiety and threat. This situation places you as counsellor in a paradox which you will need to manage carefully.

Your ability to respect your client's defences is going to be the first step towards getting beyond them. You will already have understood that psychodynamically the individual needs defences to remain intact as a person. Without them he will be unable to organize his personality and will experience disintegration and annihilation. You will also have understood that the client is likely to have developed defences early in life which, while appropriate to that phase of his development, no longer fit his present needs. In his inner world he still faces the threats which menaced his existence as an infant and he will experience these currently in the transference. He needs you to recognize and respect the quality of his defences before he will allow you to get anywhere with him. The purpose of counselling is not to leave the client without defences but to enable him to give up archaic defences in favour of something which protects and supports his current position and which hopefully may be flexible enough to allow him to develop in his life.

The client will be much aided in this rearrangement of his defences if he feels his counsellor can be trusted not to plunge him into unacceptable pain. He will experience you as doing this if you go with his resistance and seek to talk to him about the anxieties which underly his defence. Throughout the counselling relationship you will need to pay attention to the degree of rapport that exists between you and respond to the fluctuations in it. At all times the client will let you know through his resistance and defences where he experiences you as failing to hold him in a secure and reliable way.

Often the appearance of resistance may be an invitation from the client for you to address some particular issue which is giving rise to anxiety and which for the moment is causing him to withdraw. There may be times, however, when the form of the resistance is so gross that the client may be expressing his inability to engage in the counselling at all.

The counselling relationship presents the client with an opportunity to achieve something which has not been possible for him before. In the presence of his counsellor he may re-experience the anxieties which are at the heart of his conflict through the agency of the transference. With your cooperation through the counter-transference and via your interpretative activity, he may for the first time begin to put anxiety and meaning together. In psycho- ⅄ dynamic counselling we assume as the source of disturbance some failure to mediate experience, whether conscious or unconscious. This failure, which is essentially one of meaning, requires the individual to form defences which try to address the problem. However, without a context in which mediation can take place, the defences simply become fixed and the conflict remains unresolved.

/ Psychodynamic counselling presents the context where mediation may occur, because through the transference counter-transference dynamic it recapitulates the client's inner world dilemma and permits the counsellor to seek to resolve it./ You begin your work towards a resolution by first of all acknowledging your client's need to defend himself against his inner world conflicts. You continue towards a resolution by seeking to talk to your client through your interpretations about the anxiety which underlies his defence, making the links between the original source of the anxiety, its current expression in other areas of his life and its appearance between you in the transference. In this way you establish the possibility for the client of beginning to talk about something which he has not been able to talk about before. Once this has happened his defences have already been modified and a way forward has been opened.

## Case example

A young man who has run into difficulties during his first year at university is referred to a woman counsellor. His first relationship with a girlfriend has recently ended with him feeling betrayed and rejected. At his school he had been a popular and reasonably successful student and had been expected to do well. However, he now feels unsure of himself and mistrustful of his peers. Initially the counsellor feels that the recent break-up of his first relationship with a woman is likely to be a key factor in his current difficulties and seeks to encourage him to talk through his feelings of betrayal and loss. The client complies with her encouragement and talks about his girlfriend but it seems that he does so without ever managing to express any of the real feelings about her rejection. From time to time he interrupts his account to refer back to earlier times when it seemed to him that his understanding of life and control of events was almost complete.

The client is regular in his attendance and ready to talk but the counsellor begins to feel that he is holding himself beyond her reach. It occurs to her that her readiness to encourage him to explore his feelings might in itself be the focus of his resistance, since his recent rejection followed his first attempts to be open with his emotions and this had caused him much pain. She therefore changed her emphasis from trying to get him to talk through his feelings to speaking to him about his need to keep feelings out of the counselling relationship as a way of protecting himself against the anxiety he suffered whenever he felt there was a danger of losing something that had become important to him. In his assessment interview he had recounted an occasion when he was quite a young boy when he felt he had been unfairly punished for a moment of unguarded spontaneity. The counsellor was now able to link this to her understanding of his recent rejection and his resistance in the counselling by talking to the client of her recognition of his need to defend himself in the counselling against the same kind of experience of punishment and rejection that he had suffered as a boy and as a boyfriend. While this interpretation did not lead to a dramatic opening up of the work it was rewarded by acceptance on the part of the client and a deepening of the rapport between them.

---

**Key point**

The client will always seek to defend himself in order to avoid pain and preserve his sense of identity. The counsellor has to recognize the fundamental role of defences and modify her interventions accordingly.

---

# 26 Wait and wait again before responding to your client

A few years ago there used to be a television advertisement for a national newspaper the theme of which may serve to illustrate the present point. The camera shows a skinhead running along the street. The next shot is of a lone woman in a doorway. The meaning is obvious, she is about to be attacked. The youth runs past her and the camera shows a businessman a little way ahead. Clearly he is to be mugged. Then the picture widens to show that masonry is falling from scaffolding and the young man arrives just in time to push the businessman to safety. I do not know whether this advertisement was ever effective in selling more newspapers but I can think of no better example of the need to wait before we decide we know the meaning of something. This is especially true in the counselling relationship where it is so important to allow enough time for the full picture to emerge.

Psychodynamic counselling is essentially a relationship which dedicates itself to uncovering meaning in the hope that this will relieve suffering and distress. The uncovering of meaning, as we have seen, requires a framework which will facilitate it and which allows for the breadth, or perhaps it is depth, of view that is necessary. By keeping such considerations in mind, the counsellor may find it easier to hold on to her thoughts before responding to her client. It is especially important for the counsellor to restrain her responses when it is remembered that the client comes to talk not only about what he knows but also about what he does not know. As the television advertisement makes clear, too prompt a response may totally obscure the reality of what is being said and so prevent the client from reaching the understanding he needs (Winnicott, 1969).

Remaining silent and waiting for the client to say more is, however, not always an easy thing to do. This is especially so if the counsellor feels herself being drawn into a supportive role. Clearly there will be times when the pain of what the client is expressing will be such that it will be more important to recognize that than anything else. However, if the psychodynamic stance is to be maintained, space will need to be found somewhere to work with painful and emotional material with reference to the transference and to the client's inner world conflicts. Offering an acknowledgement of how painful or distressing something is rather than making an evaluative comment is perhaps the best way of indicating your presence to the client without intruding on his discourse. The counsellor needs to be able to register the ordinary human impact of the client's words while reserving a space within herself to digest what may be being said beneath the surface or in pursuit of further understanding.

In other ways clients may put pressure on the counsellor to say something before she is ready to do so. She needs to practise her resolve in maintaining an attentive silence as a way of inviting the client to recognize that the counselling is not about having a conversation or a chat, but about working together to explore and understand that which is not yet visible.

Where the counsellor does find herself responding quickly to what the client is saying and perhaps also when she finds herself tending to say rather a lot, she is giving signs of her need to defend herself against whatever may be going on in the counselling relationship. A ready and voluble response may be an indication that the counsellor is finding it difficult to maintain her stance and therefore that the containing function of the counselling is under threat. The reasons for this may be external to the relationship and relate to impingements from the counsellor's own current situation. Where this is the case she may be able to identify the distraction and recover her position by attending to her own boundaries. On the other hand, the source of the disturbance may be more internal and located in the dynamic between herself and the client. It may be that what the client is saying has triggered some defensive response in the counter-transference which is expressed in the counsellor's need to talk. Where she is able to recognize what is happening the counsellor has the opportunity to turn her attention to what may have triggered her defence and so consider what she may be reflecting in the counter-transference of the client's own conflict. She will do this by identifying her own anxiety which lies behind the defence of talking too much. Having done this she will then be able to allow the client the space that he needs rather than foreclosing on him by too rapid an intervention.

## Case example

A trainee counsellor is referred to a male therapist because of difficulties she is experiencing on the course. She is an intelligent, forceful woman with a subtly denigrating manner. Underneath her considerable presence there are feelings of emptiness and depression. The therapist experiences her as a stimulating and challenging client and often feels the need to be on his guard. The early phase of the work is marked by relatively good natured competitiveness as the client takes her time to get the measure of her man. However, as the therapy becomes more established the sessions are often characterized by an intense atmosphere of pressure as the client seeks to force the counsellor to comment. Initially the therapist tends to feel a sense of unjust accusation with a strong inclination to retaliate. However, mindful of the earlier phase of competition in the work, he realizes that he must avoid being drawn into unconsidered responses and contains his fury within himself. Typically this reticence is interpreted by the client as proof of his not caring about her and her accusations are renewed. Attempts to interpret the pattern of her attacks as relating to her anger with him for the limited nature of what he has to offer her, are royally dismissed, provoking further retaliatory impulses in the therapist. Thinking about this client, the therapist realizes that he often feels he has spoken before he is ready and yet many of his interpretations have been restrained and plausibly correct. He begins to feel frustrated at his apparent inability to hit the mark. At the same time he reflects on the level of energy that is often generated between them and the apparent contentment of the client with how things are going. He begins to see that his concern to be able to speak to the client about what she is bringing may have prevented him from paying adequate attention to what is happening between them. Somewhat belatedly he begins to see that he has allowed himself to be drawn into the therapeutic equivalent of a lovers' quarrel and that it has been the experience of this kind of intensity between them that the client has sought and not the keenness of his interpretations. It is at this point that the therapist is ready to make his first interpretation.

> **Key point**
>
> In psychodynamic counselling it is always important for the counsellor to use her therapeutic stance to give herself time and space to understand what may be unfolding and so avoid foreclosing on the client with too precipitate a response.

# 27 Inform your counselling with regular theoretical input

As we have seen throughout this book, psychodynamic counselling is an activity that requires a defined setting for it to take place. We have considered the importance of providing and maintaining the external setting as a context in which the behaviour of the client may be meaningfully understood. We have further considered the internal setting in terms of the therapeutic stance and theoretical perspective of the counsellor. Here we turn our attention to the importance for the counsellor of continuing to participate in the wider ongoing discussion about psychodynamic counselling.

Beyond her participation in the training group, so much of the counsellor's professional activity takes place within the isolated retreat of the counselling room. She maintains her part in a number of more or less ongoing therapeutic dialogues with her various clients, often without comment of a wider forum. Except when she brings her work to the marginally broader focus of supervision, she remains her client's sole partner and respondent. This being so, it seems to me to be vitally important that the counsellor should expose herself to discussion, development and debate within the psychodynamic field. Training is never an end in itself but always an introduction to a particular way of seeing or doing something. Our understanding of what takes place in therapeutic relationships or in human development is subject to review and revision, and therefore the counsellor needs to inform herself with regular input.

I remember in my own initial experience of training being somewhat dismayed to hear a seminar leader remark that it took about 10 years for the would-be counsellor to understand fully some of the more difficult theory. Whether that is literally true, I cannot say, but I think the implication that the counsellor might spend long years struggling with theory and thinking about it is not a bad description of the counsellor's relationship to her texts. I think the point is this, that to practise psychodynamic counselling, you have to expose yourself to the language and literature of that particular culture. It is not that you need theory at your fingertips as you work with a client, but you need it in your bones and in your blood, providing the vitality and the infrastructure, as it were, of your capacity to respond psychodynamically.

The practice of counselling is not simply the use of skills to facilitate disclosure or the intellectual imposition of theory to explain problems. It is a genuinely dynamic relationship involving both partners in the counselling couple at many different levels. The concept of transference counter-transference implies a richly complex meeting between the client and the counsellor. The counsellor's role in that meeting is paradoxical. Theoretically she must know what to expect. Practically she must suspend her theoretical knowingness in favour of an attentive and responsive presence. Subsequently she must combine responsiveness with knowingness in a part of herself which is free to think in order that she may finally speak to the client of what he has given her to feel and understand. As the setting provides the container for the counselling, so participation in the wider discussion of psycho-dynamic theory provides the container for the counsellor. Without her continuing to inform her work by contact with the texts of her field, the counsellor risks undermining her own capacity to think and, therefore, respond psychodynamically.

It is not just that the trained counsellor needs to continue to read. It is also important that she should continue to meet with her peers both formally, as at workshops and conferences, and informally for support. The practice of psychodynamic coun-selling is a lonely and, potentially, isolating activity, and the counsellor needs to ensure that she provides herself with a matrix within which she may find both recognition and support. In doing this she strengthens her own practice by placing it within a personally and professionally containing and supportive context.

## Case example

A female counsellor lives and practices at some distance from her training body. She has been qualified a number of years and feels confident of her grasp of the texts of her field, though it is quite some while since she last found time to do any regular reading. She is surprised one morning to receive through the post a copy of a new journal her professional body has brought out. The names of the authors of all the articles are familiar to her and she begins to flip through the pages. She is intrigued to find an article by one of her own year with whom she had enjoyed a close, if competitive relationship. She reads on. The article is called 'Reviewing the Counter-transference' and the counsellor does not expect to find anything she does not already know. However, she soon discovers theorists being mentioned whose names are new to her. She is able to follow the line of argument in the article, which she concedes is well written, but recognizes with some discomfort that her old rival is helping her to see something familiar in a different way. As she reflects on the article she finds herself applying the new perspective to a client of her own with illuminating results.

The journal contains information about a forthcoming conference on the topic of counter-transference and the counsellor decides to go. The day conference brings together some 30 of her colleagues and a tight programme of papers and discussion groups. The counsellor has prepared herself for the day by carrying out her own review of what she knows about counter-transference. As she does so she is struck by the way in which reading even familiar texts is giving her fresh insights into her current cases. The conference itself proves a challenging but energizing event and the counsellor comes away with a renewed sense of herself as a member of a profession and a somewhat chastening realization that she had been allowing herself to lose touch with the current of reflection and debate.

---

**Key point**

The practice of psychodynamic counselling requires a matrix of people, theory and discussion to underpin and inform the work of the counsellor.

---

# 28   Develop your capacity for thinking and responding at different levels

The task of the psychodynamic counsellor is by definition complex. As we take as a primary concept the relevance of the unconscious in our attempts to understand the client, we acknowledge the inevitability of having to work at many different levels. We can imagine that the counsellor and the client agree to meet each other at the level of shared reality, 'I have a problem', 'I agree to try to help you with it', 'We agree to meet regularly at a certain time for a certain fee'. This much may seem straight-forward and easy to establish. However, it is only a part of what has been put in hand by beginning a counselling relationship. At the same time we may imagine a parallel encounter between the unconscious aspects of both the counsellor and the client where a dialogue may also be established (Samuels, 1985). Thus communication may take place between the client and the counsellor, in both directions, at both the conscious and unconscious levels. So, for example, the client may present himself for counselling saying two different things.

*Client*: [*conscious level*] I have a problem. I need your help.
[*unconscious level*] I have a problem. I don't feel I can trust you.

The counsellor may similarly respond at two different levels.

*Counsellor*: [*conscious level*] You have a problem. I can help you.
[*unconscious level*] I have the same problem. Who's helping me?

Further to these communications, which we may think of as being on the level, so to speak, of the conscious and unconscious, there may be further lines of communication between different aspects of the counselling couple as well as between different aspects of each individual. Thus the client may speak from his conscious aspect to the unconscious aspect of the counsellor, or from his unconscious to her conscious aspect and vice versa. If we consider that within the unconscious of the client a number of aspects may need to address the counsellor, for example good and bad internal objects or part objects, it will be appreciated how intensely complex the counselling dialogue may be. It will also be clear how necessary it is for the counsellor to be able to listen to the client at a number of different levels as well as being able to listen to different levels within herself.

As has been implicit throughout this book, the ability to listen and respond at these many different levels will require a containing mechanism within the counsellor which will facilitate her task. A number of different factors will contribute to the internalization of such a container in the counsellor. Among these will be her training experience and intake of theory, her experience of supervision and of course her own experience in the role of client. It must also be said that the development of this capacity in the counsellor does require practice and so a counsellor should not feel too dismayed if she finds it difficult to achieve. It is enough initially that she should turn her attention to developing it. Following the cues of the client, as has been suggested in earlier sections, will provide the counsellor with her best indication as to whether she is attending to all that her client needs her to understand. Where the client fails to accept an intervention or interpretation, the counsellor needs to consider that she may have failed to attend to one level or another and that, therefore, her response is incomplete. By consulting her own thoughts and fantasies in relation to the client she may recover the level that has been ignored and incorporate it into her digestion of his material. In this way the counsellor learns how to address the client at different levels and so provide him with the opportunity to integrate aspects of himself which previously he has needed to deny.

## Case example

A young woman comes to see a male counsellor because she is disturbed by the effect on her as a child of her father's bowel condition. The man continued to suffer from colitis and his illness had frequently been experienced by her as a shameful and seemingly unavoidable intrusion on her life. As an adult she feels an obsessive need to control her relationships with people generally and is particularly anxious about the thought of relationships with men. On the surface the client and the counsellor reach a remarkable degree of agreement about the nature of her problems. Her father's frequent need to empty his bowels, it is seen, came to be experienced by her as a form of abuse, as the sound and smell of his evacuations penetrated her senses. Her anxieties about relationships generally, and about men in particular, related, they agreed, to the way in which her unconscious fantasy had come to equate faeces with penis, which therefore contaminated her image of the nature of intercourse, both social and sexual. Her continuing to live in her parents home made it difficult for her to achieve the necessary separation from her father and the beginning of independent adult life. There seemed to be little difficulty in finding areas of agreement in the work and yet the client does not manage to integrate these insights into everyday life. However, she does report feeling better about herself.

As time goes on the counsellor begins to feel that he is missing something. His attention is brought into sharp focus one day when the client reports that she has been suffering for some time from symptoms like those of her father. He is particularly disturbed to learn that if her illness fails to respond to medication, surgery is indicated which may mean a colostomy. In reviewing his management of the case the counsellor is dismayed to realize that he has been failing to take account of counter-transference responses. The apparent agreement and contentment of the client has led him to ignore those sessions when he has been left feeling switched off by the client or not knowing what to do with what she has brought him. He is concerned by the thought that the surgical option might represent a desperate attempt to deal with the faecal metaphor by cutting it out altogether and that by not paying attention to his own difficulties in digesting her material at the level of the counter-transference he may have abandoned her to the radical solution of the scalpel. He realizes that it is time to let their cosy relationship be soiled by the shit of her rage.

---

**Key point**

It is important in psychodynamic counselling that the counsellor should scan and monitor the whole of the counselling interaction and not allow herself to accept a surface reading of things.

---

# 29 Permit yourself not to know what is going on

I think one of the most difficult tasks for the new counsellor is to allow herself to enter therapeutic space without a clear sense of what might be going on. The whole thrust of a training programme is to equip the student with knowledge and clarity. The trainee is invited to account for what is going on with the client or indeed for what is happening in the whole counselling process. In the context of assessing the trainee's progress and competence to practise this may well be necessary, but within the counselling relationship itself it may be a disadvantage. Rather like the musician who must know where to place her hands to produce the right notes and yet when giving a concert forgets what she knows in order that she may perform, the counsellor has to be able to leave too much knowingness behind her as she enters the counselling room in order that she might be present to the client.

The counsellor needs to feel that she can orientate herself in the counselling relationship not by knowing what is happening but by trusting the setting she has provided, both internally and externally, to support her in her task. By observing and maintaining the framework of setting and boundaries, the counsellor provides herself with the parameters which will allow both the client and the counsellor to understand what is happening. Therapeutically it is of little value that the counsellor should know what is going on if what she knows is a theoretical import and not in tune with the client and where he is. It is better that the counsellor should herself remain uncertain until she is able to offer words to the client which permit them both to reach a degree of understanding (Fenichel, 1945). Thus it can be seen that the primary role of the counsellor when she is with her client is to involve herself authentically in the therapeutic relationship at many different levels. She does not do so apart, from the safe distance of theoretical insight, but from the much more vital and less comfortable position of inclusion of herself both as respondent to and element in the client's discourse. Where a counsellor is too anxious about her encounter with the client, she encumbers herself with theory and knowledge in the hope that this may cushion her against the impact of his need. By permitting herself not to know what is going on she abandons any tendency to omnipotent control and relies instead on her capacity for authenticity and engagement in her relatedness with others. From within the container of her therapeutic stance she has the room to observe both her client and herself in relationship. In that observing bit of herself she may draw on what she knows to reach an understanding of what is currently happening and may decide whether or not it may be timely to address the client about it.

Thus I think we may be beginning to draw a distinction between what is involved in becoming a psychodynamic counsellor, with all the acquisition of knowledge that that requires, and the practice of psychodynamic counselling with its requirement for available presence, authentic relatedness within certain bounds, and the capacity for thinking which permits the counsellor to differentiate what may be happening in the service of understanding.

With each client the counsellor has to rediscover what she knows about normal and abnormal human development or about the counselling process itself. She does this by listening attentively, and at different levels, to all that is being said between and within herself and the client. She allows themes or patterns in the discourse to remind her of things she may know but she seeks to talk to the client about these things in language which she has learned from him. Of course she borrows from other parts of her own experience, both personal and professional, but she seeks to address the client with words which belong to him, born of his inner and outer world stories. What she has learned in training and personal therapy helps her to recognize where her client may be and what he tells her about himself helps her to find the words which will fit his particular conflict. If she manages to address her client in words which make a difference for him, it is not because of what she already knows but because of what she has been prepared to learn in relation to him.

Like so many things in the field of psychodynamic counselling, the counsellor's position in relation to knowledge is paradoxical. No one would suggest that the counsellor does not need to know but at the same time not knowing may be an integral aspect of her technique.

## Case example

A qualified counsellor arrives a little late for supervision and looking flustered. She apologizes and then remarks that she does not know who to talk about today. Her routine has been disrupted and she is not sure that all her notes are up to date. Eventually she selects a client she has presented many times before and begins to speak about the last session. The client is a young woman whose boyfriend has referred her because of problems in the relationship. She acknowledges there are problems but does not find it easy to put herself in the role of client. In the session she is reporting the counsellor feels uncertain about the sequence in which the material was presented and admits to feeling anxious that maybe her client is more needy than she had at first assessed. She offers a number of apparently disjointed vignettes of what had taken place in the session.

The client had arrived looking awful and feeling apathetic, unconnected and indecisive. She has recently fallen out with a friend and knows an opportunity is coming to meet up and sort things out. At the same time there is an opportunity to do something else she does not wish to miss. Whatever she does, she feels she will have to miss out on something. She had gone on to talk of feeling small and fractured and in danger of breaking up. That's how it had been when she was younger. Her problem now was holding things together. It was difficult for her to contact people or talk to them. Perhaps the counselling was making her worse. It might have been better to leave things as they were. When she felt like this she began to question her grasp on reality.

Remembering a disclosure from the previous session the counsellor offered this remark, 'Last week you told me something important about yourself, I think that perhaps now you are feeling unsafe?' The client denied this saying that what she had said the previous week was now gone.

The counsellor was unclear about how the session had ended and was unable to say what she had felt was going on. Her main feeling now was how difficult it seemed for her to remember the session in any more detail, or to make very much sense of what she had been able to remember. It seemed clear to the supervisor that the counsellor was struggling with her counter-transference and that the primary task was to help her to reconnect with her own capacity to make links and put things together. She encouraged the counsellor to consider her discomfort and difficulty in ordering her material as itself being an element in the transference counter-transference dialogue. It was possible that the client was needing to affect her own capacity to make links, perhaps to show her what his inner world is like, or indeed to defend himself against her ability to make sense of things. In spite of her sense of being lost in the material she had in fact managed to record much of the session which she might now turn her attention to considering. While it was right to be concerned for her client, it was possible that her own anxiety was an accurate reflection of the client's anxiety about the bits of herself that seemed to get lost whenever she tried to hold things together. The counsellor began to see that by accepting her own feeling responses as elements in the discourse with her client, she could use them to speak to her about her anxiety rather than herself be overwhelmed by it.

---

**Key point**

You achieve understanding in the counselling relationship not by conscious control of the material but by allowing yourself to trust in the setting and the process.

---

# 30    Give time and space to work towards an ending

The final point to be made in this book may seem very basic and indeed it is, but I have chosen to return to a very basic issue at the end in order to reiterate what I said at the beginning. Attention to what is basic lies at the heart of developing our practice as psychodynamic counsellors.

In a sense the ending is what the client and counsellor begin work together to achieve. Viable and constructive separation leading to a successful adjustment to reality might be considered, if somewhat prosaically, the object of the counselling relationship. In that sense the counsellor must hold the idea of the ending in mind from the very beginning. The ending is not just the moment at which you and the client agree you will not see each other any more, it is the point towards which you are working from the outset.

As such it can be seen that the ending is itself an element in what we have been considering as the setting of psychodynamic counselling. Counselling must be seen as something of an interpolation in the client's life. It represents time set apart for the specific purpose of resolving that which the client has been unable to resolve on his own. He may internalize and integrate within himself important aspects of both the process and the counsellor but there will come a point when he will close the brackets and pursue the unfolding narrative of his life without the attentive listening of the counsellor. The idea of ending is therefore, a necessary boundary for the counsellor, signalling to her the temporary nature of her insertion in the client's life as well as the temporary nature of his insertion into hers. When client and counsellor meet and engage with each other with such intensity, it is helpful to be reminded somewhere of their need to part. Some metaphors for the counselling relationship speak of extremely intimate and indeed lifelong commitments, the mother with her child, or husband and wife in marriage. As useful as these metaphors may be for referring to the complexities and intimacies of the counselling relationship, they tend to obscure the reality for both parties that the relationship must end and that it is of its nature limited in what it may offer.

As we focus on the intensity of the transference counter-transference dynamic in the sessions, it is useful to remember just how limited the contact between the counsellor and the client actually is. Whatever heights or depths of emotion may be expressed within the session, the majority of our clients continue with their ordinary lives week by week without significant disruption. Separateness and, eventually, parting represent the larger container of ordinary life within which we conduct our counselling relationships.

It seems to me that we safeguard ourselves in our work with our clients if we are able to remember to anchor the work within the container of ordinary human experience. Our own need to defend ourselves coupled with the powerful expectations the client may bring to the counselling to rise beyond their limitations, act as strong magnets towards an inflated and distorted view of what we are about. Remembering the ending is a useful way of returning us to a realistic sense of what we seek to do.

Keeping the idea of ending in mind is not only helpful when thinking about the total counselling relationship, it can also be useful in regard to each individual session. Again it is possible within a session for the intensity of the encounter to distort the counsellor's sense of what she can give the client. By holding on to the idea of ending the counsellor may give herself the space she needs to reflect on what is happening. Thus the counsellor allows herself both to engage with the client and to separate out from him and in so doing anticipates the progress of the counselling relationship towards its end.

Clearly I am not focusing here on the need for the counsellor to anticipate the actual ending of the counselling relationship by allowing enough time and space to deal with it both in terms of separation and loss. I do not seek to imply thereby that these are less important. Each client deserves the time that it takes to work with the ending of the counselling relationship and the loss that it may involve. However, I have wanted to dwell more on the idea of ending as a concept which may influence our practice throughout the counselling relationship. In all that we do as counsellors we look for ways to support us in our therapeutic task and to safeguard against harming either the client or ourselves. The idea of ending can be a useful element in containing and supporting our counselling endeavour by helping us to keep our relationship with the client in perspective.

## Case example

A woman client has been in counselling for a couple of years when she begins to talk about when the relationship will end. She is particularly concerned that she should feel that she has some control about when the ending will happen and that the counsellor should not just spring it on her. Having explored what this anxiety might be about, it is agreed that the client will set her own date to bring the relationship to a close. It is early in the year and she mentions December as a time to review the date for ending. The client declares herself content with this arrangement. However, as time goes on, the progress that has previously been made appears to give way to renewed feelings of depression and despondency. In spite of the agreement that she should herself have control of the ending, she becomes convinced that it is going to happen before she is ready for it. The themes of loss and separation become central to her material. The gaps between the sessions and the longer holiday breaks become particularly difficult for the client to tolerate. At the same time any changes in the consulting room, for example, a new plant, or a renewed lampshade, provoke considerable feelings of unease in the client, as if she cannot accommodate the changes. The counsellor responds to these feelings in the client by relating them to the idea of ending and reminds the client that she is free to carry on beyond the agreed review date if she so decides. Gradually it becomes clear that although the client is experiencing considerable distress around the experience of the breaks and the idea of ending, she is in fact managing to hold her life together very well in external reality notwithstanding some very real pressures and stresses. By accepting the client's distress and occasionally reminding her of her own involvement in the timing of the ending, the counsellor helps the client in her experience of herself as dealing with her most acute anxiety, which is her capacity to survive the experience of separation and loss. By confronting the theme of ending, together with the limited nature of what the counsellor is able to offer, the client and the counsellor together provide the container within which the client's deeper anxieties can be reached and worked through.

---

**Key point**

A clear understanding of boundaries and limits allows the psychodynamic counsellor to practise effectively and appropriately.

---

# Conclusion

The points I have made in the foregoing sections which comprise the body of this book have been offered in an attempt to illustrate some of the important elements in the development of the practice of psychodynamic counselling. They have taken as their underlying premise the concept of a container within which space, both internal and external, may be considered as a context in which the discourse of the client may find meaning. From the time that Freud first heeded his patient's insistence that he should let her talk to him (Gay, 1988) the psychoanalytic tradition has learned the importance of providing a context within which the client may unfold his own narrative in relation to the counsellor. In this book I have tried to describe some of the ways in which the psychodynamic counsellor may develop her ability to do this.

In the Introduction I looked at the way we may consider psychodynamic counselling from the viewpoint of a language that may be learned and spoken. Throughout history human beings have found it necessary to tell their own story both collectively and as individuals. Telling a story in a certain context allows it to find a particular meaning and gives the individual the sense that their own experience can be understood. Whether the story has been told around the campfire, or the hearth, whether openly or in the privacy of a confessional, it has always been in the expectation that it will be heard by someone who will bring to it considered attention and understanding. In some cultures the professional listener knows that meaning will stem not simply from the telling of the story but also out of the listener's own subjective response, carrying as she does the tradition of understanding that gives a culture its own particular character.

So it is in psychodynamic counselling. Through training and personal therapy, through supervision and reading the literature, the counsellor immerses herself in a culture which brings a particular viewpoint to the understanding of human experience. She develops within herself a space for reflection which is informed by the story and thinking of psychodynamics. In developing this space she makes possible her management of external space in ways which facilitate the exploration of meaning in the unconscious. By defining and constructing a space at internal and external levels she acquires her potential for usefulness in relation to her client. She acquires a semantic framework within which she may understand her client's communications and out of which she may address him in meaningful terms. In speaking of psychodynamic counselling in terms of the acquisition of a language and a culture, I am wanting to suggest that the counsellor will find herself developing a fluency in and a familiarity with the language of psychodynamics which will eventually inform and serve her meeting with the client. The practice of psychodynamic counselling will further develop her capacity for a certain kind of availability, a certain kind of attention, a certain kind of being there, which will allow her to interact with the client at the level of his deepest need.

In Part I, Developing Work with the Internal and External Setting, I discussed ways in which the psychodynamic counsellor is quite active in fostering the provision of a therapeutic setting. To borrow from Winnicott (1963), she creates a facilitating environment, safeguarding the constancy both of the room in which she counsels and of the space within herself devoted to counselling. I invited the counsellor to think about the relationship she has with her setting and the way in which she may need to tend it and so maintain its integrity. In some respects the counsellor is required to be very practical about the disposition and management of the setting. This is no bad thing as attention to ordinary details is often a valuable anchor in a context where orientation to the nature of things may be both subjectively and unconsciously determined. In other respects the psychodynamic counsellor needs to be able to rely on the given of her setting as she allows herself to float freely, as it were, being directed not by aim or intention, but by her availability to connect with her client's unconscious. It may be seen that sensitive attention to the setting involves the counsellor in the discipline of her practice and that following that discipline will facilitate her development.

In Part II, Developing Work with Issues around the Boundaries, I began to explore the idea that the therapeutic container might need to have its limits. In the first instance, I think of limits acting as markers against which it is possible to gauge what may be happening. Because counselling is a limited activity it is possible for the counsellor to interpret the client's behaviour with reference to the boundaries. Just as borders usually define a country and in a sense enclose a culture, so the boundaries safeguard the integrity of the psychodynamic context. The boundaries, therefore, provide the objective parameters of what must essentially be a subjective activity, since it can be neither more nor less than a special kind of human relationship. Paradoxically, boundaries both facilitate and discourage. They facilitate the meeting of the counselling couple in a context which is recognizably psychodynamic, allowing both to know what is expected of them. They discourage anything, deriving from client or counsellor, which would take them outside psychodynamic territory and into an altogether different story. By tending the boundaries, the counsellor builds on her attention to the setting and underlines her invitation to the client to follow his discipline of telling his story in metaphor and symbol. By working with issues around the boundaries the psychodynamic counsellor develops her ability and skill in the practice of her craft.

In Part III, Developments in Understanding and Working with the Transference, I turned my attention to a key area in the practice of psychodynamic counselling. In a sense, transference is what makes psychodynamic counselling as such possible. Under the auspices of the repetition compulsion, the client re-experiences significant aspects of earlier relationships in relation to the counsellor. This much is easy. What engages the counsellor in much greater difficulty is developing her capacity to work with the transference. Without a sense of being comfortably located in her own therapeutic setting, the counsellor will find it difficult to work with transference. From within that setting she will find the support to receive and gather in the transference and develop her ability to mediate it. By entering a therapeutic relationship with her client, the counsellor invites transference and offers herself as its object. By remaining within her therapeutic setting, she develops the ability to respond to the client not just with feelings, but also with a capacity for thinking. Through the mediation of her counter-transference, as discussed in Part IV, Developments in Understanding and Working with Counter-transference, she acts as a bridge to the client's unconscious and thus enables and facilitates his dialogue with himself.

The concept of the therapeutic relationship in psychodynamic counselling as expressed in the dynamic of transference and counter-transference clearly envisages a richly complex and interactive partnership at both conscious and unconscious levels. I have wanted to suggest that the counsellor is responsible for fostering and maintaining this interaction and that she may develop her ability to do this by a kind of action which must not disturb her stillness. Alongside the reserve of her therapeutic stance there is the activity of her therapeutic enquiry; she feels with her client but thinks where he cannot. She may do this because her engagement in the transference counter-transference relationship is supported by her involvement in the psycho-dynamic culture. Thus the counsellor inhabits a space which defines and informs her activity. She develops her ability to work in that space by subjecting herself to the same kind of therapeutic attention that she offers her client. During the session she achieves this through careful attention to her own responses and beyond it she draws on the support of theory, peer group and supervision.

In the fifth and final part, Developments in Working with the Whole Counselling Relationship, I turned my attention to thinking about the client and the counsellor as separate and, ultimately, as separating individuals. In all the intensity of the transference counter-transference relationship, it is sometimes difficult for the counsellor to hold on to the integrity of the client's separateness, while her own may also become compromised. In developing her practice, the counsellor needs to incorporate within her setting a sense of perspective which respects the space between her and her client. On rare occasions I have had the opportunity of seeing someone I have worked with in a therapeutic setting perform in their own context, an actor, a musician or politician. It has been very important to me to witness the reality of the client's life outside my consulting room, independent of my setting and speaking with a different voice. Such opportunities allow the counsellor to hold the balance between what is internal and external in her relationship with the client and encourage her to focus on her task as a counsellor.

I hope it may have become clear to the reader that in writing this book I have not set out to dictate how she will develop as a psychodynamic counsellor. I have rather wanted to talk about the way in which I find myself thinking about how I practise psychodynamically at this point in my development. Some of what I have written has, as it were, taken me by surprise, as it has expressed itself in one point or another. The task of writing has required me to emerge from my therapeutic reverie to articulate something that by now I do without noticing, rather as I breathe. If I have used metaphors or analogies to try to express something, I have done so arbitrarily. I have not attempted to describe things as they are but as they might feel and as if they might be so. As you train and as you practise so you will develop and so you will grow your own habit of mind which will form your ways of saying what it is you do.

The title of this book begins with the word *developing*, which carries with it the suggestion of something unfinished. Psycho-dynamic counselling is not a body of theory but a specific kind of activity which takes place between two people. It is therefore, of its nature, always developing as each counselling couple discover anew the form, content and meaning of their particular inter-action. I hope the counsellor who has read what I have had to say will be encouraged to trust in the process of psychodynamic counselling and will feel that her development as a counsellor will evolve with her attention to herself as the inaugurator and guardian of therapeutic space.

# Bibliography

Bion, W.R. (1962) *Learning from Experience*. London: Heinemann.

Bion, W.R. (1967) *Second Thoughts: Selected Papers on Psycho-Analysis*. London: Maresfield Reprints.

Bollas, C. (1987) *The Shadow of the Object: Psycho-Analysis of the Unthought Known*. London: Free Association Books.

Casement, P. (1985) *On Learning From the Patient*. London: Tavistock Publications.

Fenichel, O. (1945) *The Psycho-Analytic Theory of Neurosis*. London: Routledge & Kegan Paul.

Fordham, M. (1978) *Jungian Psychotherapy: A Study in Analytical Psychology*. Chichester: John Wiley and Sons.

Freud, S. (1901) *The Psychopathology of Everyday Life*. London: Pelican Books.

Gay. P. (1988) *Freud, A Life for our Time*. London: Papermac.

Guggenbühl-Craig, A. (1971) *Power and the Helping Professions*. Dallas, TX: Spring Publications.

Guntrip, H. (1971) *Psychoanalytic Theory: Therapy and the Self*. London: Maresfield Reprints.

Greenson, R.R. (1967) *The Technique and Practice of Psycho-Analysis*, vol. 1. New York: International Universities Press.

Hinshelwood, R.D. (1991) 'Psychodynamic formulation in assessment for psychotherapy', *British Journal of Psychotherapy*, 8 (2): 166–74.

IPC (1994) *Institute of Psychotherapy and Counselling Code of Ethics and Practice*. London: IPC.

Jacobs, M. (1988) *Psychodynamic Counselling in Action*. London: Sage.

Lambert, K. (1981) *Analysis, Repair and Individuation*, vol. 5, Library of Analytical Psychology, London: Academic Press.

Laplanche, J. and Pontalis, J.-B. (1973) *The Language of Psychoanalysis*. London: Hogarth Press.

McLoughlin, B. (1990) 'The client becomes a counsellor', in D. Mearns and W. Dryden (eds), *Experiences of Counselling in Action*. London: Sage.

Malan, D.H. (1979) *Individual Psychotherapy and the Science of Psychodynamics*. London: Butterworths.

Mander, G. (1993) 'Dyads and triads: some thoughts on the nature of therapy and supervision', *Journal of the Institute of Psychotherapy and Counselling*, 1 (Autumn): 1–10.

Meltzer, D. (1967) *The Psycho-Analytical Process*. Perthshire: Clunie Press.

Rycroft, C. (1968) *A Critical Dictionary of Psychoanalysis*. Harmondsworth: Penguin.

Samuels, A. (1985) *Jung and the Post-Jungians*. London: Routledge & Kegan Paul.

Samuels, A., Shorter, B. and Plaut, F. (1986) *A Critical Dictionary of Jungian Analysis*. London: Routledge & Kegan Paul.

Sandler, J., Dare, C. and Holder, A. (1973) *The Patient and the Analyst*. London: Maresfield Reprints.

Storr, A. (1979) *The Art of Psychotherapy*. London: Secker and Warburg.

Truax, C.G. and Carkhuff, R.R. (1967) *Towards Effective Counselling and Psychotherapy*. Chicago: Aldine.

Winnicott, D.W. (1953) 'Transitional objects and transitional phenomena', in *Playing and Reality*, London: Pelican Books.

Winnicott, D.W. (1960) 'Ego distortion in terms of true and false self', in *The Maturational Processes and the Facilitating Environment*. London: Hogarth Press.

Winnicott, D.W. (1963) 'The mentally ill in your caseload', in *The Maturational Processes and the Facilitating Environment*. London: Hogarth Press.

Winnicott, D.W. (1969) 'The use of an object', in *Playing and Reality*. London: Pelican Books.

# Index